EMPLOYEL ADVOCACY:

101 CHEAT CODES

EXPERT TIPS FOR BUILDING AND SCALING YOUR EMPLOYEE ADVOCACY PROGRAM.

BY BRADLEY KEENAN

FOREWORD.

Employee advocacy is still relatively new, largely untapped, and bursting with potential impact and value: for the brands we work for, for the employees we work alongside, and for us as the individuals leading employee advocacy programs. Having launched a global advocacy program across 150 McKinsey & Co offices, I've learned that it's about more than getting employees to share a post about your company on social media every now and then. It's about empowering and inspiring each employee in your program to build a uniquely impactful presence on social media. It's about giving them the skills and tools that will enable them to meaningfully engage with their networks, make valuable new connections, and share content that builds personal and organizational credibility on social media.

It requires building widespread conviction across internal audiences and stakeholders within your organization that employee social media use brings significant value. It requires an individual or team with the energy to kickstart and develop the program over time and shout about its successes.

If you've been tapped or raised your hand to lead an employee advocacy program, you likely see the huge potential here. In my opinion, there's no more exciting area in marketing right now. Generating such considerable opportunity for impact and professional growth, running an employee advocacy program really is a job unlike any other.

I began to see the value of employee advocacy while working as a social media manager. I then followed my interest into a full-time advocacy role, at a time when that was only *just* becoming a job to be had. Even with "employee advocacy" in my formal job title at this point, I didn't know quite how to handle the challenges of launching and nurturing a large-scale advocacy program. I was still unsure what an employee advocacy program manager should actually do. How can they be successful? What skills do they need to develop?

There were, as yet, no books to read on this nascent subject or employee advocacy university degrees to study. There were no time-tested roadmaps to success or grizzled employee advocacy veterans to ask for guidance. Thankfully, I soon connected with Bradley, the best example of the latter I've found in this field.

Leading an employee advocacy program requires an entrepreneurial spirit, along with an ability to see an opportunity, build something new, and a willingness to learn as you go. Bradley embodies this. He's built companies and guided countless employee advocacy programs across industries. He knows how to launch them, how to grow them, and how to sustain them over the long haul. Bradley has big vision, but is pragmatic, and the tips in this book reflect that. All the ideas in the coming pages are immediately actionable for program managers in our position, and they are largely things you can do today - from your laptop - with little or no experience leading an advocacy program. But their collective impact, as I've seen in my many years of taking Bradley's advice, can be huge.

As an employee advocacy program manager, you get to see the fruits of your efforts every time you look at your social media feeds. You get to build something of real value to your organization, your colleagues, and for yourself. This book can help you learn what you need to get there. I am honored to be included in this book, amongst my peers from organizations around the world whose advice is referenced in the coming pages. This is the book I wish I'd had when I started my employee advocacy role, one I'm grateful to have as a resource going forward, and one I'm thrilled to share with you now.

Chelsea Bryan, McKinsey & Co.

TABLE OF CONTENTS.

LEVEL 3: A DAY IN THE LIFE 79

LEVEL 4: KILLER CONTENT 111

INTRODUCTION:
THE ONLY CHAPTER IN THIS BOOK.

Business books can be really boring. Not all of them, obviously, but I feel pretty confident in saying that many of them are... especially when written by founders of companies who have a product to sell (yes, this is me). But before you close this book and place it in the 'never to be read' section of your bookshelf, let me state my case.

Creating a book is an amazing way to establish authority and trust in your industry. It is a fantastic sales tool, as you can share the book with prospective clients. It also makes a great gift for existing clients. Not to mention the amount of social media content that you can create from the content of the book. But this is where the problem begins, and why many business books offer little value.

If you are writing about a very specific business niche, creating 15 chapters and filling 200 pages is not an easy task. We have all read books that repeat the same message over and over again.

You get to the end of the book only to realize that you spent a few hours of your life reading something, to only get a few key takeaways that you can actually use in your daily life. The book could probably have been a single social media post!

Well, this is what I wanted to avoid...

The goal of this book is simple.

Create something that gives real value, even if you only read one page.

I will give you 101 key strategies for running a successful employee advocacy program, and every single page will have genuine insights that you can take and implement right away.

But what if you don't have an employee advocacy platform?

Not a problem, all of these strategies can be implemented regardless of the technology you use (even if you do not use technology at all). So whether you have an advocacy program with 10 people or 10,000 people, there is value in every single page.

I suspect that you may be dubious and maybe even worried that I am going to use this book to sell you our product. Nope. In fact, I will only mention DSMN8 to provide relevant statistics, case studies, or resources to help you. We have launched hundreds of successful employee advocacy programs for companies of all sizes, ranging from small 100-person digital agencies to some of the largest companies in the world with over 100,000 employees, so there are plenty of learnings to share... but no sales pitch.

There are tons of books about employee advocacy programs and why you should consider it as part of your marketing mix, but this isn't one of them. I didn't feel the need to rewrite content that already existed. Instead, I'm going to take the view that if you've opened this book, you want the 'how', not the 'why'.

Anyway, enough of the preamble... it already feels like way too much waffle.

Let's jump straight into it.

LEVEL 1:

READY,
SET,
GO!

1.

CHOOSE THE MOST MOTIVATED PERSON TO RUN YOUR PROGRAM.

Your employee advocacy program won't be something you'll be able to 'set and forget'. It will require constant nurturing, so choosing the right long-term leader is imperative.

They'll certainly need to invest time upfront to launch your program, but they'll also need to commit to refining its delivery for as long as it runs. This is why it's so critical to appoint a leader with a vested interest in your program's long-term success.

Many businesses choose someone quite junior to run their program. This might seem like a logical choice, but in the long run, it often turns out to be a poor one. Running a successful employee advocacy program requires authority that a new or junior employee is unlikely to have.

The role isn't just about creating compelling social media content. Your program leader must have internal credibility, too. Advocacy from your company's senior leadership is integral to your program's success, so its leader must be able to regularly communicate with your C-level executives to bring them into your program.

But you shouldn't appoint someone too senior, either. Although a senior leader would definitely have the authority to drive your program, they might not have the time. Their other day-to-day responsibilities would likely get in the way. Senior leaders tend to make great advocates and brand ambassadors, but poor advocacy program leaders.

The right person to run your program will be someone with a few years of experience, great communication skills, an understanding of your project's goals, and the time to get the job done. Competency is key.

Over time, your employee advocacy program should come to encompass and positively impact almost every aspect of your business. You need a project leader you can trust to achieve that.

YOUR PROGRAM LEADER *MUST* HAVE INTERNAL CREDIBILITY, BUT DON'T APPOINT SENIOR LEADERSHIP – THEY'RE LIKELY TO BE TOO BUSY.

2.

GET THE FUNDAMENTALS IN PLACE BEFORE TECHNOLOGY: CULTURE + CONTENT.

Employee advocacy technology is a bit like home fitness bike technology: there are many brands, types, and features on the market... but whichever you buy, you'll still have to get on and pedal.

There are two fundamentals you'll need in place to run a successful employee advocacy program. The first is a positive culture within your organization, making employees feel safe to share content. The second is great content that employees will actually want to share.

Putting employee advocacy technology in place before those two fundamentals is a big mistake. All it will do is amplify the fact that you have no sharing culture and no content. No technology can make up for those deficiencies. Making them good is the groundwork that needs to be completed before you invest in furthering your advocacy program.

Once you have the two fundamentals in place, good technology will certainly go a long way in helping you scale it out.

Dedicated employee advocacy software helps your company manage its program more efficiently, particularly as it grows and more advocates are onboarded. The technology simplifies the process, reducing friction for all involved.

Your company will also benefit from the software's other features, such as tracking metrics. Naturally though, such features come at a monetary cost. Advocacy software is at its best when working at scale, so perhaps consider your technology choices when you are ready to have 50+ advocates involved, rather than your first 5.

Only you can decide when (or if) to invest in technology for your employee advocacy program. Just know that no amount of tech investment at any time can replace a positive culture and great content—it can only amplify the results your company is already achieving.

PUTTING EMPLOYEE ADVOCACY TECHNOLOGY IN PLACE BEFORE THOSE TWO FUNDAMENTALS IS A BIG MISTAKE. ALL IT WILL DO IS AMPLIFY THE FACT THAT YOU HAVE NO SHARING CULTURE AND NO CONTENT.

3.

GIVE YOUR ADVOCACY PROGRAM ITS OWN IDENTITY.

OK, you've got your budget approved. You're ready to go. Or are you?

An employee advocacy program isn't 'just another technology initiative'. You need to make its launch exciting to get your people on board from the start. That begins with giving your program a memorable identity.

An exciting brand-associated name—one you can include in your initial awareness comms—will connect your employee advocacy program with your company. Without one, it will just become known as "the employee online sharing thingy."

You should also come up with an exciting term for participating employees. 'Employee advocates' might sound a bit soulless. Calling them your 'insiders' or even 'influencers' may make for better engagement.

A well-run employee advocacy program is an award-worthy asset. In fact, a client of ours won a Gartner Excellence Award, due to the way they executed their employee advocacy program. By giving their program its own identity, our client's employees were able to share content about their projects in a totally unique way—something far beyond what can be achieved by just implementing some new tech.

18

Please note, app fatigue is real. The average employee uses 10 apps a day[1], so if you're going to get traction with your advocacy program, you really need to make it something special.

Taking advocacy from being just another item on your employees' to-do list to a company-wide initiative will mark that difference.

GIVING YOUR PROGRAM AN IDENTITY WILL MAKE IT MORE THAN 'JUST ANOTHER COMPANY INITIATIVE'.

---

[1] Asana (2023). The Anatomy of Work Global Index.
https://asana.com/resources/anatomy-of-work

4.

COMMUNICATE THE SHIFT TO SOCIAL.

Facebook was founded in 2004. By 2012, it had a billion users. Over those eight years, companies became pretty spooked about social media. They worried that employees might spend their days on Facebook rather than working, and wondered what might happen if they posted things they shouldn't.

So, what did those companies do? Yes, you've guessed it... They told employees that anyone posting on social media would be fired.

But as the rise of social media became unstoppable, companies started to realize the huge value of employee networks, and the concept of employee advocacy was born.

But... did anybody tell employees they would no longer be fired for posting on social media? On the whole, no.

Telling employees it's OK to post is a critical step that many companies seem to skip. This has dire consequences on employee advocacy performance.

Before you launch your employee advocacy program, make sure your employees know that using social media for work is encouraged.

EMPLOYEES NEED TO FEEL EMPOWERED BY SOCIAL MEDIA AT WORK, NOT SCARED OF IT.

5.

SOCIAL MEDIA IS WORK, SO ALLOW USE DURING WORK HOURS.

This may sound a little harsh, but if your company doesn't feel it can trust its workforce to use social media responsibly, maybe employee advocacy is not for your company.

If you're going to ask your employees to become online advocates for your business, attempting to restrict their social media activity at work is somewhat counterproductive.

Of course, you'll need a social media policy that includes guidelines on how much employees should use it. The vast majority of your workforce will use some form of social media, predominantly accessing it with smartphones.

Some of your employees are probably using social all day every day, regardless of your company's current policy. You certainly don't want to give them a license to scroll TikTok nine to five. But you do need to give advocates space to share content when they need to.

It's also worth noting that your employee advocacy program should make it easier and quicker for advocates to create content and share it, reducing the amount of time they might need to spend on social media.

12 ESSENTIAL SOCIAL MEDIA GUIDELINES FOR EMPLOYEES

1	CONFIDENTIALITY IS KEY	CLIENT LISTS, FINANCIALS, BUSINESS STRATEGIES... YOU GET IT. THESE THINGS CAN'T BE SHARED ON SOCIAL MEDIA.
2	BE RESPECTFUL	DON'T POST HATEFUL CONTENT OR ENGAGE WITH TROLLS. DON'T POST ANYTHING YOU WOULDN'T WANT YOUR BOSS TO SEE.
3	BE HELPFUL	THINK BEFORE SHARING. IS THE POST YOU'RE SHARING EDUCATIONAL, TOPICAL, OR INFORMATIVE? IF NOT, RECONSIDER.
4	FACT-CHECK BEFORE POSTING	ESPECIALLY WHEN USING AI WRITING ASSISTANTS, BE SURE THAT ANY STATISTICS YOU SHARE ON SOCIAL MEDIA ARE CORRECT.
5	FOLLOW & ENGAGE WITH OUR CHANNELS	WE WANT TO BUILD A THRIVING COMMUNITY ON SOCIAL, SO PLEASE DO FOLLOW AND ENGAGE WITH OUR CONTENT!
6	TAG US IN YOUR SOCIAL MEDIA BIOS	FOR EXAMPLE, YOU MIGHT PUT "MARKETING @DSMN8" ON TWITTER. MAKE SURE YOUR LINKEDIN SAYS WHAT YOU DO + WHERE.
7	FOLLOW OUR BRAND STYLE GUIDELINES	WHEN CREATING CONTENT ABOUT OUR COMPANY, FOLLOW OUR STYLE GUIDE. IT COVERS THINGS LIKE FONTS AND COLORS.
8	RESPECT BOUNDARIES	SOME OF YOUR COLLEAGUES MAY NOT WANT YOU TO SHARE A PHOTO OF THEM ON SOCIAL MEDIA. RESPECT THEIR BOUNDARIES.
9	USE SOCIAL MEDIA AT WORK, BUT DON'T SPEND ALL DAY ON IT	SOCIAL MEDIA IS A FUN PLACE, BUT IT CAN BE EASY TO LOSE TIME SCROLLING. DON'T LET IT TAKE OVER YOUR DAY.
10	CYBER SAFETY IS ESSENTIAL	ALWAYS USE STRONG PASSWORDS AND 2-FACTOR AUTHENTICATION. DON'T SHARE YOUR PASSWORD WITH ANYONE.
11	WHEN IN DOUBT, ASK!	IF YOU'RE NOT SURE ABOUT SOMETHING, GET IN TOUCH WITH YOUR MANAGER, THE SOCIAL MEDIA / MARKETING TEAM, OR IT.
12	REMEMBER OUR COMPANY VALUES & CODE OF CONDUCT	WHETHER ONLINE OR IN THE OFFICE, WE EXPECT EVERYONE TO ADHERE TO OUR CODE OF CONDUCT AND COMPANY VALUES.

6.

CREATE AN ADVOCACY-READY SOCIAL MEDIA POLICY.

Your social media policy should outline the code of online conduct you expect your employees to adhere to. This includes the behavior you expect from them when sharing anything online, work-related or not.

If you're as old as me, you'll likely recall social media policies that read, in essence, "don't ever share anything on social media, full stop."

In recent years, companies have come to realize that having employees actively posting and engaging on social media can be hugely advantageous. This evolution has led to policies becoming far more inclusive and encouraging.

The goal of your social media policy should be to guide and support employees, not police them. If yours is a big list of things not to do, it's going to make them too scared to post anything.

Instead, align your policy with business goals. Present it as a tool to empower your employees, enabling them to use social media to help the company meet those goals.

A clear policy that states what's completely off limits, while allowing for authentic posting, will both alleviate employee worries and help you avoid a PR nightmare.

It's imperative to make sure employees are aware of your new social media policy. They need to know that times have changed. Give copies to new starters as soon as they join.

Your social media policy should enable your team to use social media to your company's benefit, not create barriers to stop them.

Use my free social media policy template to get started.

7.

SEND PROGRAM INVITES FROM THE MOST SENIOR PERSON POSSIBLE.

When you invite people to your employee advocacy program, you'll want to have the biggest impact from the outset. Naturally, there's a difference in how many people will sign up if a junior HR manager were to send the invites vs., say, your CEO. People rarely ignore emails from their CEO.

You may not be able to get the CEO to send the invites, but you should certainly try to find the most senior person in the organization that would back the project. That way, when people receive the invite, they don't just ignore it. You can even start by inviting department heads and have them invite their own teams.

We see that when somebody in a C-level executive position invites people to an advocacy program, there's around a 30% increase in the number of people who sign up.

This also sets the tone for the program going forward. It shows that the employee advocacy program has C-level support as a strategically important company initiative, and that management expects staff to engage.

It also works really well if the invites coincide with an event, such as an all-hands meeting or a company update. Mention it in the meeting, then send the invites immediately after.

" WE PILOTED EMPLOYEE ADVOCACY WITH OUR EXECUTIVE TEAM, AND THEY ABSOLUTELY LOVED IT! THEY WERE THE PERFECT ADVOCATES FOR OUR COMPANY-WIDE ROLLOUT. EACH LEADER SENT A PERSONAL NOTE TO THEIR TEAM, SHARING THE BENEFITS ADVOCACY BRINGS TO INDIVIDUALS AND OUR COMPANY. THEIR SUPPORT REALLY AFFIRMS THE VALUE OF OUR PROGRAM, AND WE SAW STRONG ADOPTION RATES."

LEAH PETERS, DIRECTOR OF SOCIAL MEDIA, FRONTIER*.

*FRONTIER IS A LEADING TELECOMMUNICATIONS PROVIDER IN THE USA.

8.
"IS THIS THING ON?!":
SEND PROGRAM INVITE REMINDERS.

Eventually, you'll be ready for employees to join your advocacy program. But when that big day arrives, how will you invite them?

Email is the most common method, and it can work very well. But sometimes recipients are busy, working on an urgent task, or on holiday when an email arrives. Many unexpected emails go unopened and are eventually discarded.

Sending invite reminders makes a big difference. You don't want to bombard people with emails, but sending up to 3 reminders over a few weeks really will boost your numbers.

It's best to make your reminders friendly nudges: pushing too hard will be counter-productive. A simple, "You might have missed this the first time around, but lots of other people have already signed up—we'd love you to join them..." will be fine.

Highlighting how employees will benefit from joining your program will make your reminders even more effective. Include some success stories—or even better, mention some employees who have already become advocates. Sometimes people just want to know the initiative they're joining is already well-established and successful.

Bradley Keenan 🏃 (He/Him)
Founder & CEO of DSMN8. The Employee Influencer Platform. Grow yo...
2h · 🌐

Don't make this mistake ✖

Let's say you're starting an employee advocacy program.

You invite your colleagues to join.

A few of them sign up.

Then... nothing. Tumbleweed.

One of the WORST things you can do is forget to send invite reminders.

Recruiting for your program needs to be ongoing. So don't just send out one email then never mention it again.

Some people will inevitably miss that Slack message or email, they'll be on holiday, or just generally busy. That doesn't mean they won't join in the future.

Take it a step further by getting key stakeholders to send those invites. Onboarding your sales team? Get the Head of Sales involved.

Employees need to know that this isn't just a marketing fad, it's an initiative backed by senior leadership, a shift in your company culture.

9.
FAILING TO PLAN IS PLANNING TO FAIL... CREATE A GAME PLAN!

Trying to launch an employee advocacy program without a detailed plan is akin to starting a long, complex journey without knowing your destination or how you're going to reach it.

You need a plan.

There are simple yet vital decisions to be made ahead of your program's launch. For example, you'll need to work out exactly who will participate. And with the many benefits of an employee advocacy program, it's likely that many of your company's departments will want to be involved—each one with its own agenda.

Start by defining your goals. Answering these three basic questions will help you to get your advocacy program on the rails and moving in the right direction:

First, **what are you hoping for from your advocates?**

More web traffic? Thought leadership? The development of an employer brand? No matter what you're aiming for, make sure it is the North Star in your decision-making process.

Second, **who will you invite to become advocates?**

Single business units within your company? Specific teams? Specific regions? Everybody? Knowing which employees you'll target first helps focus your strategy and communications.

Third, **what content will you have ready to go?**

Your advocates will need content to post as soon as your program is under way, and you'll need to be consistent in creating more. Make sure you know where your content will come from in the future.

There's nothing worse than announcing a new initiative, but not having all the pieces of the puzzle ready. Without an idea of where it's going and what it's trying to achieve, it will be far too easy for your employee advocacy program to become derailed.

Listen to the Masterclass with Katherine Keenan, Talent Brand Program Manager at Dropbox, to learn her top tips for the first 30 days of your employee advocacy program.

10.
GET SET TO SPREAD THE WORD: CREATE A COMMS PLAN.

Your employees should be excited by the upcoming launch of your advocacy program, not surprised by it.

Employees are more likely to ignore an email regarding a subject they know nothing about, as they may assume it's not relevant to them. Expecting them to sign up to your program on its launch day when they've been caught off-guard is a bit unrealistic. You'll need to make employees aware of your program and educate them about its goals way ahead of launch for it to hit the ground running.

Start off by explaining the benefits of personal branding and why the advocacy program is important. Create a communications plan to tease its launch, letting them know they can expect it soon. Giving your employees time to process and understand this information will help generate a buzz of pre-launch excitement. Think of it as awareness communications.

Your formal invites should be the final step of your communications plan. If your employees are surprised by them, it's probably because your communications plan has failed, meaning your program will be slow to start.

EMPLOYEES NEED TO KNOW WHAT ADVOCACY IS *BEFORE* YOU INVITE THEM TO JOIN A PROGRAM.

11.

CREATE PERSONAS FOR YOUR POTENTIAL ADVOCATES TO BEGIN TO UNDERSTAND THEM.

In sales, we talk about buying personas. It's essentially creating a fictional representation of an ideal customer in order to better understand their needs.

So apply that concept to employee advocacy. What are your potential advocates like?

To get you started, I've built 4 personas based on the types of people that make good advocates. Understanding their different motivations, challenges, and content preferences before launching will help you shape your program to drive advocate engagement.

1. The Seller
This is the most obvious one, but they aren't necessarily a salesperson. It's anyone in the company with quotas to reach. Their main challenge is time. They're under pressure to hit their numbers. Their motivation to join an advocacy program would be to exceed targets by positioning themselves as thought leaders. The content that resonates with this person helps them make sales. It'll be things like social proof, case studies, product updates, and industry news.

2. The Leader

The CEO, divisional heads, and sales leaders all have an external responsibility to show what's going on in the company, and an internal responsibility to lead employees. Their challenge is engaging the workforce. They're time-poor, and although social media may not be their number one focus, their motivation is to be seen as industry experts while broadcasting company communications, internally and externally. The content that will work for them will be customer success stories, company news (acquisitions, senior leader appointments, mergers), case studies, and financials.

3. The Champion

This is someone who loves where they work. They support the company mission, believe in it, and want to be an ambassador. Their challenge is internal politics. For example, they might not go on LinkedIn and write content about their company, out of fear of stepping on marketing's toes. They're afraid of getting it wrong. They also don't want their employer to think they're looking for a job by building their personal brand. Their motivation is simple: they enjoy being a cheerleader for the company. The content they lean towards is positive PR, awards, and company culture.

4. The Ambitious

These people are looking to advance their career by networking and building their personal brand. Whether they believe in the company mission or not is irrelevant. They know that sharing content makes them more visible, both internally and externally. It makes them look like a team player and boosts their reputation. This person's challenge is that they're dependent on their digital reputation. They need content to share, and lots of it. They don't have a content preference.

12.
NOW ESTABLISH YOUR 'IDEAL ADVOCATE PROFILES'.

Next, use the table opposite to create 4-5 'ideal advocate profiles'. They are the people in your company that you believe employee advocacy will help the most. Not the people that can help you the most. Your initial thoughts might lean towards sales, marketing, and recruitment, but let's go deeper. What are these people like? What are their goals? Why would they want to join your program?

Creating these advocate profiles will help you to focus on the value to the person you're selling to. If you launch your advocacy program saying, "Please, join our advocacy program because it'll really help the company", it would be like Apple saying, "Please, buy our new Mac because it'll make us money". It's not going to work. You need to demonstrate how advocacy will alleviate their specific pain points and help them reach their objectives.

Using ideal advocate profiles in the planning stages will help you to efficiently target prospective advocates by tailoring your messaging. It will also help you decide how to approach that person or group to improve the probability that they will sign up.

When you're considering the best way to approach potential advocates, be sure to identify the key stakeholders who might be a gateway to that group of people. They're the ones with influence, e.g. the VP of Sales. Know how you're going to communicate with that individual and show why advocacy should be important to them too. Get them on side and watch your program grow!

Learn more in <u>episode 36</u> of the podcast, and download the PDF worksheet using the QR code.

Who?	Business Objectives / North Star	Pain Points	How Does Employee Advocacy Help?	Content Preferences / Special Notes	Key Stakeholder
Salespeople	Make sales, generate leads, reach quotas.	Time, growing their network, positioning themselves as thought leaders.	Helps them build a social media presence while saving time finding and creating content.	Product information / updates, sales content, industry news.	VP of Sales.

13.
PROVIDE A 'GET STARTED WITH SOCIAL' KIT.

For your advocates to be effective, they'll need to feel they're presenting the best version of themselves.

Creating your own 'get started with social' toolkit is a great way to give all employees the necessary guidance to confidently engage with your program. Your toolkit might include, for instance, advice on how best to take a profile picture or write a LinkedIn biography. Access to your social media policy, and social media communication training is a must. Much of it may seem obvious to you, but that won't mean it is to them.

Your toolkit might also give company brand guidelines regarding LinkedIn header images, job formats, and titles— to ensure all your advocates' profiles adhere to a consistent style. You could also create templates to streamline the process.

Make your 'get started with social' toolkit available to all employees, either through your company intranet, or as part of your new-starter pack. This will make sure all advocates are on the same page.

6 ESSENTIALS FOR YOUR 'GET STARTED WITH SOCIAL' KIT

◆ Your social media policy.

◆ Your brand style guide, e.g. typefaces, color palettes, logos, and tone of voice.

◆ Social media guidelines, covering things like how to behave professionally online, and cyber security.

◆ Guidance on how to optimize their LinkedIn bios and how to take professional profile pictures.

◆ Your brand social media channel usernames and hashtags.

◆ Where employees can find support, e.g. a Slack channel, and first point-of-call for social media issues.

14.

PEOPLE ARE BUSY! MAKE SHARING CONTENT EASY.

Your employee advocacy program will need to make sharing content simple. Don't, for example, bury all your content in some hidden SharePoint drive where your advocates can't find it.

If content isn't easily accessible, people won't share it. Everyone is busy, so make it easy for advocates to find the content they want to share. Don't make them go searching for it; it should only be a click or two away.

If you have a lot of content, you may need to create 'content buckets' relating to employee roles. This prevents advocates from needing to sift through everything to find something relevant to them. Think about the content you're going to produce. If some of it will only be relevant to certain business units, make it easy for those advocates to find.

Segmenting your content means the right content will be shared by the right people.

You should also provide advocates with options for their posts—different captions and images, for instance. Again, make it easy for them to select the content that best matches their personal brand and what they are trying to achieve by sharing.

Utilize your existing technology to help advocates find content. Your internal communication tools will be great for notifying them when there's new content available to share.

The easier your program is to use, the more likely it is that somebody's going to participate—and not only once, but time and time again.

DON'T BURY YOUR EMPLOYEE ADVOCACY PROGRAM DEEP WITHIN ANOTHER PLATFORM OR INTRANET.

MAKE IT EASILY ACCESSIBLE.

15.
A STRONG PERSONAL BRAND IS PRICELESS. MAKE SURE EMPLOYEES KNOW THAT!

One of the biggest reasons people don't post on social is that they're worried it might harm their careers. Employees worry that if they suddenly start posting, their managers and co-workers might think they're looking for a new job.

To counter those worries, you need to promote the benefits of employees developing strong personal brands—and carry out that promotion at a company level. Encourage all your employees to share, and explain why they should. That way, they'll feel safe and happy to do so.

You might be worried that helping your employees create their own personal brands could make them more attractive to other companies, potentially resulting in them being headhunted. But actually, employee personal branding will not only hugely benefit your business and its image, but also make it more likely to retain and attract talent.

Employees with strong personal brands have stronger relationships with their social media audiences. This results in those audience members having stronger relationships with *your* brand. Employees with well-developed personal brands can also become seen as thought leaders and industry experts, building further trust and kudos within their networks.

Providing content to your employees to help their personal brands flourish will be a vitally important part of your advocacy program. You'll need your employees to feel empowered to post more about what they know. This, in turn, results in more posts about your company.

Key Benefits of Personal Branding For Employees:

Boost Your Career by demonstrating expertise. Stand out on job applications and when going for promotion!	**Grow Your Network** and develop professional relationships.	**Make Your Job Easier** (especially in sales, marketing, or recruitment).
Upskill. Learn digital content creation, writing, and social media. Digital skills are in demand!	Become a **Thought Leader,** the go-to person for expert knowledge in your industry.	**Opportunities** like getting invited to events, interviewed on podcasts, or even featured in the media.
Empowerment. You have a voice, you're not just a cog in the machine.	**Increase Your Visibility Internally**, especially with Senior Leadership.	**Connect With Your Colleagues.** Engage with their content, and support each other.

16.
DISCOVER THE CONTENT THAT RESONATES MOST WITH EMPLOYEES.

Marketing teams know what works for your corporate pages, but not necessarily for employee profiles. Trust that your advocates know their networks. They know what content is best to share with their own audiences.

Bear in mind that this will vary from department to department. The content that resonates with sales leaders isn't going to be the same as engineers, for example.

Find out which posts are being shared by your advocates most frequently. Do they fit a particular pattern or a theme? Are they sharing videos more than images or text?

You'll also be able to compare the engagement they receive on different kinds of posts. Employee advocacy program leaders and content marketers can use this information wisely.

The easiest way to maintain results is to create more of the content that resonates with employees. Advocates will be more likely to share it, and their audiences more likely to engage.

I'm not saying don't try new things, because obviously you should, but don't try to fix what isn't broken.

THE EASIEST WAY TO MAINTAIN RESULTS IS TO CREATE MORE OF THE CONTENT THAT RESONATES WITH EMPLOYEES.

17.

LEAD BY EXAMPLE: EMPLOYEE ADVOCACY STARTS WITH YOU.

You're probably not going to want to hear this, but you should never consider yourself above participating in your own employee advocacy program. You need to lead by example!

Maybe you work in marketing and communications. You already know how to post on social media, so you might think you don't need an employee advocacy program to encourage you... It doesn't matter.

Because if you are going to ask people to participate in an initiative to share content for the company they work for, you yourself need to be a participant... Even if you do not believe you would add value or need the support yourself.

The last thing you want to hear from a new potential advocate for your program is, "why should I do it when you don't?"

Become advocate number one.

Bradley Keenan 🏆 (He/Him)
Founder & CEO of DSMN8. The Employee Influencer Platform. Grow ...
1yr · 🌐

The 🔑 to Employee Advocacy - Lead from the front!

Now, this might not be a very popular thing to say,

but we work with many marketing teams and there's a common theme that marketers tend to subscribe to,

and that is, that some of them think that they're actually above needing to use an employee advocacy tool themselves. 🙄

they feel like this is something that they can do by themselves.

However, the statistics just do not support that.

I looked at the finance sector. Specifically in the US with companies with over a thousand employees

and on the whole, about 6% of people are regularly sharing content on LinkedIn.

Now when you filter that and actually look at people who just work in marketing the statistics do not change a huge amount.

It goes to about 10%. So,

yes, that's a big leap on the 6%. But still, 90% of people who work in marketing roles are not actively sharing content on LinkedIn.

Now, beyond the fact that you as a leader who's launching an advocacy program may or may not need to use it yourselves,

by demonstrating to your ambassador network that this is something that you yourself do on a regular basis will make a big difference when it comes to user adoption. 🚀

The last thing that you want as an advocacy program leader is to be seen as somebody who doesn't use the product yourself.

So you really have to live it to encourage others to participate.

LEVEL 2:

SELECT YOUR CHARACTERS

18.

DON'T WASTE YOUR TIME TRYING TO CONVERT NON-BELIEVERS AT FIRST.

Have you ever seen two sports fans argue about whose team is best? It's pretty much a pointless conversation; they're never going to be convinced by the other person.

Ask people to become part of something new, and naturally, you'll get pushback. I say, there's no point trying to convert atheists, and that couldn't be more true when it comes to employee advocacy.

If you ask somebody to join a program to help them share content on social media and they give you a huge amount of pushback, it's probably because they haven't invested much time in building their network. Therefore, their audience may be of little to no value to you anyway.

However, that won't always be the case: some employees will have an audience but not be convinced by your program. The best way to convince them of its efficacy will be to show them evidence of their colleagues using company content to grow their own personal brands. Once they've seen that, they'll probably join when it suits them.

As with all new products and services, your program will have early joiners and laggards. Don't spend too much time trying to convince skeptical employees to become advocates.

Instead, focus your efforts on empowering those willing to participate. If your company has employees that are social media savvy enough to be posting company content already, finding and inviting them to become official advocates is a great place to start. This will save you a lot of time and energy when kickstarting your program.

Use the 'Pyramid of Employee Influence' below to figure out who to target first. Initially, don't bother trying to convince the bottom two groups: the 'not engaged', and the 'curious, but not looking for more work'.

THE PYRAMID OF EMPLOYEE INFLUENCE:

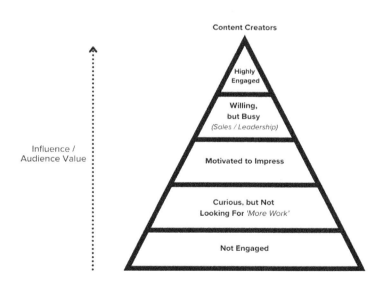

19.

MAKE ADVOCACY PART OF EMPLOYEE ONBOARDING FROM DAY ONE!

Constant employee turnover means constant advocate turnover, so never stop looking for new advocates.

Find out what your employee turnover rate is. You'll need to find new advocates at the same rate to prevent your advocacy program shrinking. If you aim to grow your advocacy program way beyond your employee turnover, it should naturally offset any shrinkage.

Be sure to approach every new employee. New employees will want to demonstrate their commitment to your company and impress their new colleagues.

Once they've become advocates, they're also more likely to stay advocates: having joined your program on their first day, they're likely to feel it's part of their core responsibilities.

Turning new employees into advocates is most easily achieved by including program sign-up in your new employee 'starter pack'. Include your platform sign-up link if there is one and if not, the links to all your amazing content.

Once implemented, these steps will save you time by creating a consistent stream of new advocates.

STEP 1: FIND OUT YOUR COMPANY EMPLOYEE TURNOVER RATE.

STEP 2: FIND NEW ADVOCATES AT THE SAME RATE (OR ABOVE) TO AVOID THE PROGRAM SHRINKING.

STEP 3: MAKE SURE ALL NEW HIRES ARE AWARE OF YOUR PROGRAM FROM DAY 1!

20.
ENCOURAGE PARTICIPATION, BUT DON'T FORCE IT.

Don't try to push your employees to advocate. **Do** enable them to make social media part of their roles.

Clearly, the more advocates your company has, the more potential ROI your program can deliver. But trying to force employees to become advocates by mandating it across your company is pointless.

First, it will turn advocacy into just another task on your employees' 'to-do' lists, discouraging them from investing properly in your program. Advocacy programs—and brands —can be damaged by advocates posting carelessly.

Second, employees with valuable networks are likely to quickly understand the importance of advocacy and want to get involved. If an employee has to be pressured into becoming an advocate, it's unlikely they're the owner of a useful network anyway, so why bother?

If you believe your program won't get good results without a company-wide mandate to advocate, your company is probably not ready to launch an advocacy program.

" IN EMPLOYEE ADVOCACY PROGRAMS, ENCOURAGING PARTICIPANTS BRINGS MORE VALUE THAN MANDATING IT. AUTHENTICITY EMERGES FROM WILLINGNESS, NOT COMPULSION. FORCED INVOLVEMENT TRANSFORMS A POTENTIAL OPPORTUNITY INTO AN UNWANTED CHORE WHICH DOES NOT WORK WELL WITH ORGANIC GROWTH AND THE PERSONAL CONVICTIONS OF YOUR EMPLOYEES."

JULIAN WACHOWIAK, CORPORATE CAMPAIGN MANAGER, COSMO CONSULT GROUP.*

*COSMO CONSULT GROUP IS A PROMINENT IT SERVICES AND CONSULTING COMPANY BASED IN BERLIN, GERMANY.

21.
EVERYONE INFLUENCES SOMEONE. DON'T BE TOO PICKY.

Regardless of the size of their network, every advocate in your organization will be able to influence someone.

There is no reason to be picky about which employees you invite to join your program. The more advocates your program has, the more successful it will be, so let everyone who wants to advocate get involved. With the right encouragement, an advocate with only 50 LinkedIn connections could become your company's next thought leader.

Yes, some of your C-suite advocates might get at least 100 reactions every time they post, whilst some of your interns might only get one—but that one reaction might be from your next customer.

And don't forget about the network effect.

A post from an intern might resonate enough with a larger influencer for them to re-share it with their own network, suddenly making that intern's post visible to thousands of potential clients.

" WE ALLOW EVERYONE IN OUR BUSINESS TO SUGGEST CONTENT, AND OFTEN FIND THE PEOPLE WORKING CLOSELY WITH THEIR LOCAL COMMUNITIES HAVE THE MOST TO ADD."

ALBERT BUNGAY, CONTENT MANAGER, IWG.*

*IWG IS THE WORLD'S LARGEST WORKSPACE NETWORK, OPERATING IN 6 CONTINENTS, WITH OVER 8 MILLION PEOPLE USING THEIR WORKSPACES.

22.
RECRUIT, ONBOARD, AND RECRUIT SOME MORE!

It might seem an impossible goal, but you should aim to make every employee of your company an advocate. You'll probably never achieve 100% adoption, but don't let knowing that stop you from trying. As your advocacy program grows over time, more employees will see its success, and the more success employees see, the more they will want to share in it.

It's very common for an organization to have less than 5% of its employees as advocates, and for those few to be posting content on LinkedIn alone. So if, through continual recruitment, your program reaches only 20% adoption, it could still mean a 300% increase in the social activation of your company. Not a bad headline, right?

Your goal should be to make your advocacy program a staple within your company, something that all employees are aware of, whether they have joined it or not.

I see many companies stop trying to onboard more advocates when they achieve a self-designated goal of, for example, 500 advocates. This is a mistake. Don't stop onboarding. The more advocates the better.

Once your program reaches about 1,000 advocates, it's likely to snowball, with more and more employees becoming advocates without any additional effort from the program's leaders, until it becomes self-sustaining.

This is particularly prevalent in larger enterprises: employees hear about their company's advocacy program from their colleagues or team leaders and join without being invited, simply because they want to. This snowball effect is the ultimate goal of inviting employees to join your advocacy program.

EMPLOYEE TURNOVER MEANS THAT YOU NEED A CONSTANT FLOW OF NEW ADVOCATES TO MAINTAIN AND GROW YOUR ADVOCACY PROGRAM. STARTING A "REFER A COLLEAGUE" INCENTIVE WITH PRIZES HELPED US SPREAD THE WORD ABOUT THE PROGRAM ACROSS THE BUSINESS AND DOUBLE OUR ADVOCATE NUMBERS IN JUST A FEW WEEKS!"

MARTA KEDZIERSKA, MARKETING COMMUNICATIONS SPECIALIST.

23.

NO ONE *REALLY* KNOWS WHO THEIR MOST POWERFUL ADVOCATES WILL BE.

Our clients tend to think they have a pretty good idea of who their most influential advocates will be before their programs have launched. Client-facing employees and senior leaders are obvious nominees.

Marketing and sales team members will also see clear and immediate benefits of being active on social. Though, this is not the whole picture... far from it, in fact.

In pretty much all cases, we find employees in non-client-facing roles with massive networks of relevant people.

It's entirely possible that many of your company's employees have worked at other companies in your industry during their career, building relationships along the way—and not just with co-workers. Their contact list might include members of the press or even the CEO of your largest client.

There is no need to be precious when considering who to invite to your advocacy program. Encourage anyone who wants to join. You may find some hidden influencers in your company's ranks.

Bradley Keenan 🏃 (He/Him)
Founder & CEO of DSMN8. The Employee Influencer Platform. Grow yo...
24m · 🌐

When starting an employee advocacy initiative, most program leaders will have ideas around who would be their best advocates.

Typically, they are:

- Senior Leadership
- Sales & Marketing
- Those in client-facing roles

Take this a step further by creating ideal advocate profiles before inviting your first advocates. Highlight how advocacy helps them reach their KPIs and overall business goals.

But that doesn't mean you should limit your program to JUST those people.

Initially, you'll want to get those ideal advocates on board. Then, open up the gates, and invite the rest of your organization.

Who knows, you might discover that an intern in your team is a hidden influencer.

And don't ignore non-client-facing roles.

Think about it this way:

A software developer is likely to be connected with other people in their field. If they're someone with 5 or 10 years experience, their network could be vast. Next time you're hiring a software developer, they'd be the perfect person to share that job opening.

Don't miss that opportunity by only inviting your ideal advocates. Invite them first, then encourage everyone in your company to join.

24.
HEAR ME OUT: ADVOCACY ISN'T JUST FOR EMPLOYEES.

It's called an employee advocacy program, but that doesn't mean everyone needs to be an employee. Employees won't be the only ones with a vested interest, after all. Your program could be set up to encourage everyone who might benefit from your company's success to advocate for it, no matter who they work for.

Board members and investors tend to make great advocates, often having extensive networks through which they can spread your brand message.

Your company might work with agencies, consultants, partners, and resellers—any or all of whom could become valuable advocates. Why not reach out and ask if they would be interested in sharing content about your brand?

Your company may feel it's appropriate to create different content or captions for non-employees to share, but it's not universally necessary.

About 4% of all users across our employee advocacy programs are not direct employees of the companies running them. A network of external advocates operating within your program can be really, really beneficial—so don't automatically restrict advocacy invitations to your employees.

7 EXTERNAL CANDIDATES FOR YOUR ADVOCACY PROGRAM:

 BOARD MEMBERS

 INVESTORS

 CONSULTANTS

 AGENCIES

 RESELLERS

 PARTNERS

 SERVICE PROVIDERS

25.
GO OLD SCHOOL: PROMOTE YOUR ADVOCACY PROGRAM IN PERSON.

Methods like company-wide emails can be an effective way to promote your employee advocacy program, but they're also easy to ignore. Sometimes 'old-fashioned' in-person methods are more effective.

They can have an amazing impact, breaking the norm of receiving yet another email and making it clear that your program is an important company project. Posters, desk drops, and even pop-up stands in common areas can really boost awareness. A display with a QR code linked to your sign-up page is a relatively inexpensive way to drive interest.

It's also worth encouraging senior leadership to mention the program in company-wide meetings. Creating regular updates for your company's leaders will enable them to enthuse about advocates' social media activities, showing your employees it's something leadership cares about.

Some of our clients host really successful 'Lunch and Learn' events to explain the benefits of being social media active to their employees. I'm sure the coffee and donuts don't hurt the attendance figures! This blend of physical world, face-to-face communication, and digital methods will take your employee advocacy program's recruitment to the next level.

4 WAYS TO PROMOTE EMPLOYEE ADVOCACY IN PERSON

1. Conduct a 'Desk Drop'

Let employees know about your program by leaving a gift on their desk, alongside an informational flyer about the new initiative and how they can join!

2. Create a Display

Whether it's a poster or a display stand, make it clearly visible. Explain what the program is, and include a QR code for people to sign up.

3. Lunch and Learn

Host 'lunch and learn' sessions to educate employees about advocacy, improving their social media presence, and how to create content.

4. Social Events & Company-Wide Meetings

Away-days and company-wide meetings are a great opportunity for promoting advocacy. Encourage employees to take photos at social events for content.

26.

COMPANY CULTURE IS *EVERYTHING.* EMPLOYEES THAT FEEL VALUED WILL NATURALLY BECOME ADVOCATES.

Company culture is the foundation of employee advocacy. Employees that feel valued are much more likely to naturally advocate for your company, and want to join your program!

To put it bluntly, employee advocacy cannot exist without a good company culture. Forcing employees to post positively about your brand on social media when they don't want to isn't the way to go. The content simply won't come across as authentic, and employees will begrudge you for making them do it.

A thriving company culture encourages collaboration, creativity, and an atmosphere of trust. You'll want honest feedback on your advocacy program content in order to improve it, and you'll only get this in an environment where employees feel safe to voice their opinions.

Focus on improving your company culture, and you'll see better results from your program.

" A COMPANY IS PEOPLE ... EMPLOYEES WANT TO KNOW... AM I BEING LISTENED TO OR AM I A COG IN THE WHEEL? PEOPLE REALLY NEED TO FEEL WANTED."

RICHARD BRANSON, BRITISH BUSINESS MAGNATE, AND FOUNDER OF VIRGIN GROUP.

27.

LEAVE NO ADVOCATE BEHIND: SOME WILL NEED MORE GUIDANCE THAN OTHERS.

It's quite likely that some of your advocates will already be social media veterans with high levels of digital dexterity. Whilst your program will add fuel to their fires, they won't really need much education or encouragement from it.

In contrast, some of your other advocates may be very new to the idea. Employees in the early stages of their careers, who've only just created their business social media accounts, perhaps. Or maybe a member of your C-suite who's not yet aware of the business benefits of social media.

Some of your company's employees, though keen to try it, may even be 'non-digital natives' for whom social media may not come naturally.

But needing some time and encouragement to get to grips with using social to benefit their career doesn't make an advocate any less valuable to your company.

Bear in mind that an advocate's network size isn't necessarily the defining factor of their effectiveness. A CEO with 500 LinkedIn connections can quite often outperform an influencer with 10,000—because the relevance of posts is a more important key factor.

An advocate in the early stages of their social media journey might need not only program-user training, but also mentoring in growing their network. It could take face-to-face training to get them on track, or just the provision of resources for them to read and learn from. Whatever it takes, every one of them will be worth your investment.

" ENCOURAGE ADVOCATES TO PERSONALIZE THEIR CONTENT AS MUCH AS POSSIBLE, BY ADDING THEIR OWN FLOURISH TO SUGGESTED CONTENT. BUT MAKE SURE THEY KNOW THAT DOESN'T MEAN THEY NEED TO WRITE THE LONGEST OR MOST OPINIONATED POST! WE'VE SHARED TIPS ON OUR INTRANET TO SUPPORT OUR ADVOCATES, COVERING EVERYTHING FROM USING EMOJIS TO OUR TONE OF VOICE."

SARAH RUZGAR, GLOBAL HEAD OF COMMUNICATIONS, AWIN.*

*AWIN IS A LEADING GLOBAL AFFILIATE MARKETING PLATFORM.

28.
RECORD YOUR TRAINING SESSIONS.

Employee advocacy training is vital. You'll need to ensure your employees understand not only how to advocate, but also why they should want to.

Training sessions will give your employees the chance to ask questions about the processes involved in successful advocacy, helping you to create an FAQ list and a dialed-in onboarding process.

Don't expect to be able to reach everyone you'd like on the same training call, especially if yours is a large company. Yet running a training session for one or two employees each week isn't a good use of time, and one session a month might result in employees losing interest after waiting too long to join.

You can alleviate some of these issues by recording your training sessions. Making edited versions of these videos available to potential advocates will save you time and give you the ability to onboard employees at a faster rate. This makes it much easier to scale your program.

WHAT TO INCLUDE IN TRAINING SESSIONS:

1. Where Employees Can Find Your Social Media Policy, Assets, and Content To Share.

This will be your employee advocacy platform if you're using one, or a dedicated intranet folder if not. Make sure new employees all receive access!

2. Professional Social Media Etiquette

Teach them how to be professional online, including how to network, and what not to do. Remind them that they need to follow your company code of conduct. Keep it positive, you're not trying to scare employees off!

3. Social Media Platform Training

Don't assume all employees are social media savvy. Some might need more guidance than others. Cover the platforms you want employees to use. Show them how to optimize their profiles for visibility.

4. Content Creation Best Practices

The fun part: creating content. It's best to get your marketing team onboard for this one, as they know your brand voice the best! Share examples for inspiration.

29.
TIME IS MONEY: DEMONSTRATE HOW ADVOCACY HELPS SALESPEOPLE HIT SALES QUOTAS.

Onboarding your company's salespeople is likely to be a little more complicated than onboarding other employees. You may have to take a slightly different approach.

Assuming salespeople are all about money is a rather stereotypical view. Money is unlikely to be their sole focus, but the nature of their work and professional environment means it's likely to be an important factor in their working lives.

To a salesperson, time is money. A salesperson you invite to advocate might feel you're asking them to give up their time for something that's not a priority for them—so be sure to explain how they can use the program to help them hit their sales quotas.

You might, for instance, remind them that being active on social media and sharing content aimed at their target markets will mean they're at the front of prospects' minds when they're ready to purchase. You might also direct them to the swathes of information assets and courses about social media's positive impact on sales.

Make sure you align with your company's sales leaders first, though. You'll need to ensure they share your vision of using social media to increase sales opportunities and nurture existing pipelines before you start onboarding their employees.

Your sales team members have all the tools needed to become thought leaders. They'll be able to share product information, industry insights, and knowledge to make potential customers believe it's your company that has the answers they're looking for.

Of all your company's employees, it's the salespeople who will benefit most from a successful employee advocacy campaign. Make sure they know that.

REMIND THEM THAT BEING ACTIVE ON SOCIAL MEDIA AND SHARING CONTENT AIMED AT THEIR TARGET MARKETS WILL MEAN THEY'RE AT THE FRONT OF PROSPECTS' MINDS WHEN THEY'RE READY TO PURCHASE.

30.
SPREAD THE WORD! LET ADVOCATES INVITE THEIR COLLEAGUES.

Just like a good marketing campaign, a good employee advocacy program will have a viral component.

It's likely that employees outside of your program will see your advocates sharing content and ask how they can get involved. The social proof of seeing one of their colleagues doing so well on social media may be just what's needed to make them decide to throw their hat in the ring. Hopefully, your advocates will be happy to explain the benefits of the program to curious colleagues!

You could offer advocates a tangible incentive to onboard new advocates, but in most cases, it's unnecessary. People like being facilitators of success.

Allowing advocates to invite other employees to join will reduce not only your program staff's workload but also the friction involved in onboarding. So, create an environment in which advocates feel safe and encouraged to invite colleagues, and aim to make it as easy as possible for those potential new recruits to join.

3 REASONS TO LET EMPLOYEES INVITE THEIR COLLEAGUES:

1 REDUCE WORK FOR PROGRAM LEADERS / ADMINS.

2 PEOPLE LIKE BEING FACILITATORS OF SUCCESS.

3 IT HELPS BUILD A COMMUNITY AROUND ADVOCACY.

31.
MORE PEOPLE = MORE RESULTS. THINK BIG.

It is easier to reach a large audience by scaling up your program throughout the company, rather than limiting it to a specific group.

You'll want to onboard your senior executives, sales team, and marketers first... but there's no need to stop there.

I have seen companies limit their program to exactly 100 advocates as part of a particular group, and refusing to allow more to join. It was a one-in, one-out policy. The results from those top 100 advocates were great, as they had been hand-selected, but the results would have been even better had they brought everyone in.

It's not a complicated concept. The more advocates in your program, the more resource you'll be able to command, and the greater the reach of your content.

It's also worth remembering that advocates' networks will differ by size. Whilst your CEO may have tens of thousands of LinkedIn connections, one of your interns may only have 50 or 60. Although sometimes it's the other way around!

Employee audiences will naturally have a bit of overlap, but that's just a tiny percentage of their networks.

Having a diverse range of advocate networks working in tandem will actually help your program reach its goals. Keep in mind that not all content is relevant to all people. It's bad practice to have everyone share everything. You'll want to make sure the right people share the right content.

More content creators.

More results.

More influence.

More support from leadership.

WHILST YOUR CEO MAY HAVE TENS OF THOUSANDS OF LINKEDIN CONNECTIONS, ONE OF YOUR INTERNS MAY ONLY HAVE 50 OR 60. ALTHOUGH SOMETIMES IT'S THE OTHER WAY AROUND!

LEVEL 3:

A DAY IN THE LIFE

32.

LINKEDIN FEED FULL OF YOUR COMPANY CONTENT? DON'T WORRY, YOU'RE NOT OVERDOING IT.

When you first launch an advocacy program, your social media feed might seem overwhelmed with posts from your advocates. You might feel you've overdone things, and that there are just too many people sharing your company's content.

Don't panic!

Naturally, as an employee advocacy program manager, you'll be connected with lots of your colleagues on social media. So when they post, it'll show up in your feed.

Also, social media algorithms are largely determined by whose content you engage with, which is likely to be your co-workers. Therefore, as advocates start to share content, the algorithms will serve you that content.

It's important to consider that other users won't have the same feed as you. If you want to get a more realistic view of your program's output, make your feed view chronological.

Our research shows network overlap is typically less than 5%, so it's not something that should worry you. Nonetheless, it's definitely something to be aware of.

You can help combat overlap by asking your advocates to share content at different times, thus spreading out its distribution.

Remember: if your feed gives the impression that too many advocates are sharing content, it probably means your advocacy program is working well.

" BECOMING WELL KNOWN (AT LEAST AMONG YOUR PROSPECTS & CONNECTIONS) IS THE MOST VALUABLE ELEMENT IN THE CONNECTION PROCESS."

JEFFREY GITOMER, SALESPERSON AND AUTHOR OF 17 BESTSELLING BOOKS.

33.

ROME WASN'T BUILT IN A DAY: THE KEY TO COMMUNITY BUILDING IS CONSISTENCY!

Think about your advocacy program as a community.

The thing about building a community is that it takes time. You can't expect a thriving advocacy community from day one.

Yes, there's likely to be initial excitement and participation, but your program needs nurturing to maintain that level of interest.

There's no use in inviting all of your current employees, and then forgetting to invite new recruits. Do this, and your program will inevitably die with staff turnover. Consistently invite existing and new employees to participate.

Hype up your advocates! Be sure to thank them and shout out their successes. Engage with their content, offer support, and celebrate their wins. This is something that should be done on a regular basis, to keep them engaged and feeling appreciated.

The same goes for content! If you're using a platform, you'll want to make sure there's a bunch of content from a variety of sources (e.g. your company blog, YouTube channel, third-party articles) loaded in before inviting employees. Otherwise, they'll log onto an empty page and think, "well, no one cares about this", and never use it again.

There's also no use sharing an abundance of content initially, only for it to become stale in a few months. Regularly curating and maintaining content is crucial.

That consistency is integral. Otherwise, employees will either forget about it, or have the impression that it isn't important to the business, and not bother participating.

MAKE SURE THERE'S A BUNCH OF CONTENT FROM A VARIETY OF SOURCES LOADED IN BEFORE INVITING EMPLOYEES. OTHERWISE, THEY'LL LOG ONTO AN EMPTY PAGE AND THINK, "WELL, NO ONE CARES ABOUT THIS", AND NEVER USE IT AGAIN.

34.
GOOD THINGS COME TO THOSE WHO WAIT, SO BE PATIENT.

Advocacy does not happen overnight.

It's important to understand that even if you onboard hundreds of advocates straight away, it will take time for them to grow strong networks and build trust on social media.

Results may not be immediate, but as you continue to invest in the program, you will see the impact unfold.

Not all employees will be fully engaged from the beginning, so you'll need to factor in time to onboard and train them.

Dedicate regular time each week to nurturing and advancing your advocacy program. Consistency is crucial— if you stop putting in the effort, progress will slow down or halt.

Your strategy shouldn't be a prison, so give it room to evolve and adapt. Initial trial and error will help you discover what works best for your organization. Embrace patience and persevere; with time, your employee advocacy program will thrive.

NOT ALL EMPLOYEES WILL BE FULLY ENGAGED FROM THE BEGINNING, SO YOU'LL NEED TO FACTOR IN TIME TO ONBOARD AND TRAIN THEM.

35.

DON'T WORRY ABOUT THE INITIAL DROPOFF. IT HAPPENS TO EVERYBODY!

As with all initiatives and pieces of software, employee advocacy tends to have an initial spike in interest when implemented. It's the brand new thing in your company! People will start sharing straight away, as they're excited to take part.

This is inevitably followed by a dropoff in activity. Don't panic, it's normal. It's how you recover from the dropoff that matters.

Consistency is fundamental, particularly in the first weeks of a program. Maintain interest by encouraging and supporting advocates, giving them shoutouts, and congratulating them.

What's even more important is to make sure there is plenty of content available for your advocates to share on a regular basis. This will keep them engaged, and more likely to regularly check for new content to share.

Track employee participation and provide ample opportunities for feedback and support to avoid any future dropoffs. Continue inviting new advocates, and make sure your advocacy program is explained to new recruits during their onboarding.

3 WAYS TO MAINTAIN INTEREST:

1 CONSISTENTLY PRODUCE CONTENT

INTEREST IN ADVOCACY WILL DECLINE IF YOU STOP
PRODUCING CONTENT REGULARLY. EMPLOYEES
SHOULD KNOW HOW MUCH CONTENT YOU
PRODUCE, AND HOW FREQUENTLY YOU PRODUCE
CONTENT.

2 CELEBRATE THE WINS

CONGRATULATE EMPLOYEES ON THEIR
ACHIEVEMENTS, AND SHARE REGULAR UPDATES ON
THE RESULTS OF YOUR PROGRAM, FOR EXAMPLE ON
A MONTHLY BASIS.

3 CONTINUE RECRUITING

YOU MAY HAVE AN INITIAL TARGET OF HOW MANY
EMPLOYEES YOU WANT TO ONBOARD. BUT DON'T
STOP THERE! CONTINUE RECRUITING, AND MAKE
SURE ALL NEW HIRES KNOW ABOUT IT.

36.
CAP IT: LIMIT YOUR EMPLOYEES' DAILY SHARES.

You want employees to be excited about the launch of your employee advocacy program, and obviously, you want them to participate. But you do need to be wary of them being over-eager and sharing everything in sight.

New advocates may be lacking in social media experience, and if you've created an exciting program encouraging them to share in order to succeed, they may think that the more they share, the more successful they'll become. So it's always a good idea to have a content sharing limit.

If an advocate shares 10 times a day, it's going to look bad to their audience—and that will be bad for your company and its brand. It could also negatively impact the credibility and reputation of your program, reducing the number of potential advocates.

Nobody wants to join a program that carpet-bombs social media with repetitive content.

You need advocates to be sharing quality content with their networks, in order to generate engagement. But you don't want them sharing for the sake of sharing.

The average user of our platform shares 2.2 pieces of content a week, which is OK... but one post a day per advocate is probably the sweet spot.

Two a day is actually quite a lot, and our research shows that sharing more than three times a day actually has a negative impact on engagement.

AIM FOR 1 POST PER DAY
2 IS PUSHING IT
3 IS FAR TOO MUCH!

37.
PUSH REALITY VIA DIGITAL: PROMOTE IN-PERSON EVENTS.

Employee advocacy isn't just about sharing content. Your advocates can promote essentially whatever you (and they) like.

When it comes to defining what employee advocacy fundamentally is, to put it simply, it's word-of-mouth marketing.

Aside from social media, where else do we see word-of-mouth marketing thrive?

In-person events. They're the old-school way to build interest in your product or services, as well as grow your personal network. Many business leaders nowadays have moved away from in-person events to things like digital webinars. We have the opportunity to do both, so do both. Don't shun one for the other.

Here's why you should promote in-person events via your employee advocates:

Their audiences will be the kinds of people you want to reach and see at your events. After networking online with your advocates, meeting them in person will further cement the professional relationship, and build trust in your company.

Consider the flip side, too; your advocates can connect with people on LinkedIn that they met at one of your events. Now they're going to see your company content, having already established trust with one of your advocates!

Don't forget that people have more influence and reach than brands online. Your advocates will be able to get people in seats far easier than a post on your company social page or an email will.

SOCIAL MEDIA + IN-PERSON EMPLOYEE ADVOCACY = THE BEST OF BOTH WORLDS.

38.
EVERYONE HAS AN OPINION, SO DON'T FEAR BAD REACTIONS.

Don't let occasional bad reactions from your audience discourage you from continuing your employee advocacy program.

An important piece of marketing or PR content generating some negative comments might make you think social media advocacy is a bad idea for your company—but don't overreact. In my experience, such comments are few and far between.

Yes, social media can be a scary place; you never can tell when a troll might pop up. But trolls are often just like badly-behaved children. They're only doing it for attention, and if you give them attention...

You get the idea.

As part of their social media training, your advocates should be encouraged to ignore trolls and disregard negative comments without responding. That's usually the best course of action.

You won't want your advocates getting into online arguments because their professional contacts may be watching.

MAKE SURE YOUR ADVOCATES KNOW TO IGNORE TROLLS. PROVIDE SOCIAL MEDIA TRAINING SO THEY KNOW HOW TO BE PROFESSIONAL ONLINE.

THE LAST THING YOU WANT IS YOUR EMPLOYEES BEING SEEN ARGUING ON SOCIAL MEDIA.

39.
KNOW WHEN YOUR AUDIENCE IS ACTIVE AND POST WHEN IT COUNTS!

As the optimum sharing time varies from network to network, you should educate your advocates so they can make their own informed choices about when to post.

Geography and time zone are the obvious key factors in engagement, but they're far from being the only ones.

For example, advocates should also consider avoiding posting at times their connections are more likely to be in meetings, e.g. 9 am on a Monday morning, and perhaps avoiding posting on Mondays and Fridays altogether, as those are usually the busiest days for executives.

Weekends can be great for engagement, with high levels of interaction—but because many people will be scrolling for entertainment rather than to find business solutions, weekend posts will often result in less traffic being directed to your company's website.

BEST TIMES TO POST ON LINKEDIN:

You'll want to test and find out what works best for you, looking at your LinkedIn analytics. But, as a starting point, Hubspot research[2] suggests these times for posting company content on LinkedIn, per industry:

- **Software and Media:** Weekday mornings, and outside of traditional working hours.

- **Higher Education and Healthcare:** Weekdays from mid-morning to early afternoon (10 am – 2 pm).

- **B2B Businesses:** Weekdays in early mornings, during lunch, and during commuting times.

- **B2C Businesses:** Weekdays during lunchtime (12 pm – 2 pm), and outside of traditional business hours.

---

[2] https://influencermarketinghub.com/best-times-to-post-on-linkedin/ Data Source: Hubspot Report, last updated Jan 2023.

40.
PROMOTE JOB ADS WITHOUT SPENDING A DIME.

People know people who know people.

Your advocates are highly likely to be connected to people who work in the same fields they do... who are also highly likely to be connected to other people who also work in those same fields... As a result, your employee advocacy program could be extremely useful for attracting new talent.

You might want to hire new engineers, for example. If so, encouraging your engineer advocates to post about the benefits of working for your company can really pay dividends, attracting potential new employees at a fraction of the cost.

But you shouldn't expect simply blasting social media with job ads to bear fruit. Talent acquisition through employee advocacy needs to be delicately balanced with content promoting your company as a desirable workplace.

It doesn't need to be complicated. Content that features a tour of your offices, existing employees discussing their experiences, or pictures from team away days will all help provide that balance. Potential candidates who've been primed by your advocates' posts are far more likely to hit the 'apply' button on your job ads.

"WE PUBLISH OUR JOB ADVERTISEMENTS ON RELEVANT PLATFORMS AND ALSO DIRECTLY ON LINKEDIN. HOWEVER, WE ALSO USE OUR EMPLOYEES BECAUSE THEY HAVE THE RIGHT CANDIDATES IN THEIR CONTACTS AND A JOB SUGGESTION FROM A WELL-KNOWN PERSON IS MORE CREDIBLE THAN AN ADVERTISEMENT."

MARIJANA SLADIC, DIGITAL CONSULTANT, SWISS POST.*

*SWISS POST IS SWITZERLAND'S PUBLICLY-OWNED POSTAL SERVICE, AND THE SECOND LARGEST EMPLOYER IN SWITZERLAND.

41.
TRUST YOUR PEOPLE! THEY KNOW WHAT THEY'RE DOING.

Micromanaged advocates are not authentic advocates.

Yes, it will be a good, valuable practice for your program to offer your advocates templated text for captioning their posts—but captions created by your advocates, naturally demonstrating their own unique points of view and vocabularies, will always be more authentic and thus more powerful.

Your advocates aren't just experts in their own fields—they're experts at being their authentic selves, too. Rather than risking killing creativity and alienating your advocates and their audiences, your leaders should take the time to thoroughly communicate your program's vision and goals, and then leave your advocates to post in ways that highlight their authenticity and expertise.

Empowering your advocates to write their own post captions, source their own content, and even invite their co-workers into your program will go a long way toward creating the most credible and effective program possible.

" AT KANTAR, WE LIKE TO EMPOWER OUR PEOPLE WITH CREATIVE FREEDOM. TRUST IS INTEGRAL TO OUR EMPLOYEE ADVOCACY PROGRAM APPROACH, SO WE DON'T MICROMANAGE OR COMMAND PARTICIPATION."

SHA GORUR, GLOBAL HEAD OF DIGITAL CONTENT, KANTAR.*

*KANTAR IS A PREMIER DATA, INSIGHTS, AND CONSULTING COMPANY BASED IN LONDON, UK.

42.

INTERNAL COMMS AND EMPLOYEE ADVOCACY ARE NOT THE SAME.

Yes, internal communications will always be inherently linked to your employee advocacy program. They'll both always involve employees and communication, but their objectives are very different.

Internal communication is almost the step *before* employee advocacy. Its purpose is to distribute company internal content to employees, in the hope they'll digest it. This makes them aware of what's going on inside their organizations, as well as enabling them to communicate and collaborate.

The purpose of an advocacy program is to encourage and empower employees to take content produced for external consumption, and amplify it using their own professional social media connections. The tone of external content is very different, as it's designed to ultimately win new business, promote a brand, educate an industry, or find talent.

That means you'll probably need to appoint someone from outside your internal comms department to run your advocacy program, someone with the skill set and knowledge required to create an excellent social media post. One of your internal communications workers may have that ability, but it will likely be by chance. This is

100

because social media content creation is very different from the internal comms core competency of educating a workforce.

Your aims should be to build an employee advocacy program that serves both your company and your external audience—and to build it by working in partnership with your internal communications department. When you launch your program, it's likely some people will be confused and take it to be an internal communications initiative. Be prepared to help them understand by highlighting the marketing elements that define employee advocacy.

To find out what impact employee advocacy has on internal communications, my team analyzed over 1,000 employee social media posts[3]. The results were fascinating. Over 37% of interactions on social media posts containing company content came from co-workers. Using external channels as a way to reach your workforce is an added bonus of advocacy!

WHAT IMPACT DID 1,000 EMPLOYEE SOCIAL POSTS HAVE ON INTERNAL COMMUNICATION?

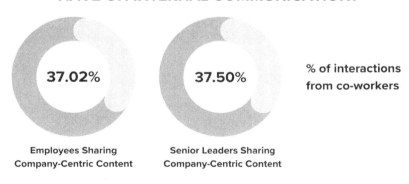

37.02%

Employees Sharing Company-Centric Content

37.50%

Senior Leaders Sharing Company-Centric Content

% of interactions from co-workers

3 https://dsmn8.com/blog/bridging-the-gap-internal-communications/

43.
SHARING IS CARING! RE-SHARING IS... NOT.

Ideally, your company's advocates should share original content by posting directly to their own profiles.

While re-sharing still has its place and some value, overall it's a far less effective way to share.

Your employee advocacy program must educate your advocates about the value of peer-to-peer sharing. Simply put, social media users trust content written by someone they know way more than they trust corporate content. In fact, peer-written content generates more than 10 times the engagement.

Your program will be far more effective if it uses, original content—not just re-shares—regardless of who wrote the originals.

CONTENT WRITTEN BY YOUR ADVOCATES (OR PRE-WRITTEN BY MARKETING/ADVOCACY PROGRAM MANAGERS) GENERATES OVER *10X MORE ENGAGEMENT* THAN 'RE-SHARES'.

44.
INTEGRATE...
BUT ONLY WHEN IT ADDS VALUE.

Have you ever heard of "demo code?"

You may not have, but I'm going to let you in on a little secret... Technology companies sometimes create features or integrations that they know customers will never use, simply because they look good during demos. Prospects often ask for features or integrations they think they'll need, but once the tech is live, turn out to be unnecessary.

Rather like that situation, you might think it's necessary to integrate your employee advocacy program with every aspect of your business, but that's a lot of work and you probably don't need to.

Yes, you'll want to make it as easy as possible for employees to join your program and find content to share. But you'll need to consider where to integrate and where not to.

For instance, integrating employee advocacy with your reporting system and internal communications platform will allow you to track important metrics and notify people when there's new content available.

But keep in mind that the core objective of your employee advocacy program is to share content externally. Integrate it too deeply, and that core objective may become lost.

The key goal is to make it easy for people to access your program, without burying it among other applications that could cause it to be sidelined or forgotten.

BE STRATEGIC WITH INTEGRATIONS.

TRACK IMPORTANT METRICS, AND MAKE IT EASY FOR EMPLOYEES TO PARTICIPATE.

THE REST IS UNNECESSARY.

45.

ADVOCACY WORKS IN REGULATED INDUSTRIES.
YOU JUST NEED TO ADJUST YOUR STRATEGY.

There's no denying that regulated industries have it harder when it comes to social media. In pharmaceuticals, finance, oil and gas, and legal services there are a lot of rules and regulations you need to follow.

Add employee advocacy into the mix, and it might just seem too risky for leadership to endorse the concept.

But what if I told you it can be risk-free?

Employee advocacy works incredibly well in regulated industries, as long as you adjust the strategy to make it appropriate. Here's what to do:

Instead of encouraging employees to create their own content, get your marketing team to create it for them. Provide pre-written captions for employees to share, ensuring legal compliance and preventing the distribution of misinformation.

You'll see the benefits of employees being active online, without giving your board members a heart attack over rogue social posts.

Limit your advocacy program to professional social media platforms that you conduct business on, particularly LinkedIn. Onboard your C-Suite to set a positive example for the rest of your team.

Most importantly, make sure your social media policy outlines the do's and don'ts. Provide all the necessary training to make sure everyone understands how to behave professionally online.

Listen to podcast episode 28 to find out more about advocacy in regulated industries.

> ❝❝ **EMPLOYEES CAN BE WORRIED THAT THEY MIGHT SHARE THE WRONG THING. THOUGH THEY'RE FREE TO EDIT THEM, WE'VE SUGGESTED FROM THE START THAT THEY STICK WITH ONE OF THE PRE-WRITTEN CAPTIONS, WHICH ALLEVIATES ANY WORRY THAT THEY MIGHT SAY SOMETHING THEY SHOULDN'T.❞**

PATRICK CANTELLOW, DIGITAL MARKETING MANAGER, KNAUF.*

*KNAUF IS A MULTINATIONAL BUILDING MATERIALS COMPANY BASED IN GERMANY.

46.

GET A BOOST FROM WITHIN: ENCOURAGE ENGAGEMENT ON COMPANY POSTS.

Some of your employees will be less forthcoming than others in their approach to social media. But encouraging all your employees to advocate at some level will be a win-win.

Although they might not be up for sharing content from their own accounts, advocates with a more introverted disposition will probably engage with posts from your company's corporate social accounts. Encouraging them to like or comment on other advocates' posts will be worthwhile too, increasing the visibility of those posts and boosting their impact.

Now, your less extroverted advocates probably won't be looking to become LinkedIn influencers, but their engagement will still be hugely valuable, trackable, and rewardable—so why not give them the opportunity to engage?

Doing so might mean all of your employees will want to join your program and engage at their own comfort level, regardless of individual attitudes. Perhaps those who are only lacking in confidence will be able to engage less actively until their confidence grows. Then, eventually, they'll be more likely to become fully-fledged, creative advocates.

> " **DEMONSTRATING THE VALUE OF THE CONTENT SHARES FROM OUR PEOPLE CERTAINLY HELPED WITH ONBOARDING OTHERS. KNOWING THAT THEY ARE PLAYING A KEY PART IN DRIVING VALUABLE TRAFFIC TO OUR PLATFORMS, AS WELL AS INCREASING THEIR OWN VISIBILITY ON LINKEDIN, HAS HELPED US WITH EMPLOYEE PARTICIPATION.**"

STEPHEN FARRELL, SENIOR DIGITAL COMMUNICATIONS SPECIALIST, AKZONOBEL*.

*AKZONOBEL IS A MULTINATIONAL PAINT AND PERFORMANCE COATINGS COMPANY BASED IN AMSTERDAM.

LEVEL 4:

KILLER CONTENT

47.
AVOID FUTURE HEADACHES: DON'T OVERCOMPLICATE CONTENT SEGMENTATION.

If you're going to create content specific to certain aspects of your business, creating 'content buckets' for different company departments, business units, and regions will help advocates find and share content that's relevant to them. It's a process that will be well worth the effort.

It might look like an overwhelming task when you consider your organization's departmental and geographical structure, and all of the ways in which your content could be segmented—but, in fact, too much segmentation will create more work and more complications anyway.

It'll be better to start with a simple program content structure and apply segmentation only when and where it becomes necessary. If all your content is going to be written in English to begin with, there'll be no point in creating a bucket for content in Spanish on day one, for instance. Avoiding any such over-complications will save you a lot of headaches.

Start to apply segmentation when you've built up a lot of content. Focus on making it easier for your advocates to find relevant content, so they won't feel overwhelmed.

However, employees often love supporting their colleagues in other regions and departments, so don't make it difficult for advocates to draw from other content buckets.

Allow all your advocates access to all your content, and give them the autonomy to share whatever they feel is relevant to their audiences.

EXAMPLE CONTENT BUCKETS:

48.

SCHEDULE CONTENT AHEAD OF TIME. YOUR FUTURE SELF WILL THANK YOU.

Every social media manager knows that scheduling content way ahead of time is the best policy. You'll need to adopt the same approach with your employee advocacy program.

Creating a content calendar will enable you to schedule higher-quality content when it matters most. It also makes it easy to rearrange schedules to accommodate posting new, time-sensitive content to reflect current events.

Naturally, the time spent creating and organizing content will increase as the size of your program increases. Allow for this when planning your program.

A consistent output of content for advocates to share is fundamental for maintaining results and interest in your program.

But don't overwhelm yourself with creating 'new' every time. Repurpose your older content and share third-party articles, too.

LISTEN TO MY <u>PODCAST EPISODE</u> ON SCHEDULING ADVOCACY CONTENT:

49.

CATEGORIZE & DEFINE YOUR CONTENT SOURCES CLEARLY.

It can be daunting to think that you need to curate every single piece of content for your employee advocacy program before people share it. This is a common misconception. You'll want to add content as you go, so it's up-to-date and as fresh as it can be. This doesn't apply to evergreen content, but we'll get to that in tip #61.

In 99% of cases, when content is going into an employee advocacy program, it is already in the public domain. It has already been signed off and published.

Before you launch your program, create a ledger of content sources—the places where you are already regularly publishing content. This could be obvious things like your company news page, blog, or YouTube channel, but it could also be third-party content sources, whether it's Forbes magazine or trade press specific to your industry.

Once you've created this list of content sources, map them to the business units, whether that's geographies, departments, or service lines. You want the right content going to the right people. Providing relevant content to your employees is incredibly important—you want to provide value, so making sure they have access to hyper-relevant content will go a long way.

Where possible, it is worth automating the process of that content coming into your employee advocacy program. This will reduce the time it takes to source relevant content. Using RSS feeds, dedicated advocacy software, or content aggregation tools can assist with this.

3 STEPS TO DEFINING & MAPPING YOUR CONTENT SOURCES:

1. Create a list of everywhere you publish company content.

For example, your company social media accounts, YouTube channel, blog, company news page, podcast, email or print newsletter.

2. Add third-party resources.

What publications are the go-to source for news and insights for your industry? Create a list of these for your advocates to share content from.

3. Get the right content to the right people.

Map your content by geography, language, or department. Your engineers won't want to share the same content as the sales team!

50.
KEEP IT REAL!: DON'T WRITE POSTS LIKE A COMPANY SPOKESPERSON.

Your employee advocacy program should help your advocates develop their own social media brands—not just parrot the company line and relay corporate messaging.

It would be fantastic if every advocate created all their own posts, using their own turns of phrase to add their unique and valuable insights... but that's a little bit unlikely, so your program will need to provide them with authentic-sounding content instead.

And, in fact, if your program's content makes them sound more like digital billboards than authentic advocates, it's less likely they'll want to sign up in the first place.

So make sure your advocacy content is different from what's on your company page and website. It needs to read as if written by a credible advocate, rather than a corporate copywriter on a rinse-and-repeat cycle. Content and captions that read with authenticity will not only win more engagement but also help your program grow.

Create content that will help your advocates connect with their audiences. It will pay dividends in the long run.

" IF PEOPLE LIKE YOU THEY WILL LISTEN TO YOU, BUT IF THEY TRUST YOU, THEY'LL DO BUSINESS WITH YOU. "

ZIG ZIGLAR, AMERICAN WRITER, SALESPERSON, AND MOTIVATIONAL SPEAKER.

51.

IT'S NOT ALL ABOUT YOU: KEEP YOUR CONTENT VARIED.

Using your employee advocacy program to communicate your sales message will probably be fine, as long as it's done well.

Creating gated content to secure contact details, so a salesperson can immediately try to win business, is probably doing it badly.

Not everybody who looks at your content will be in a buying cycle at that point. Your program's content should reflect that, and take the opportunity to create trust for your brand by educating the market and providing insight into your company.

You might, for instance, decide to spotlight your employees by celebrating promotions, weddings, and births. Creating educational content to enhance people's understanding of your industry and how they might do their jobs better can also be an effective tool.

That way, when those people are looking to buy, they'll think of your company as a trusted advisor.

Think of each article of your program's content as belonging to one of these three categories:

Company-Centric Content

Focus on your company's products, announcements about quarterly results, and other items directly associated with your company.

Employee-Centric Content

Spotlight your employer brand and company culture by focusing on employee away days, new appointments, and internal initiatives.

Third-Party Educational Content

Emphasize your employees' expertise, and also feature industry news, best practice guides, and third-party reviews.

I recommend that your content should be one-third company-centric, one-third employee-centric, and one-third educational content from third parties.

52.
DON'T BE SCARED OF EMOJIS.

A simple emoji really can add emotional impact to a page of text.

I realized the truth of that quite recently and I'm now a bit of an emoji convert, but it's taken me a while to get there.

The first emoji was created in 1999 by Japanese artist Shigetaka Kurita, who worked on the development team for 'i-mode,' an early mobile internet platform from Japan's main mobile carrier, DOCOMO. Their rise in popularity, if not ubiquity, saw the 'face with tears of joy' emoji become the Oxford Dictionary's 'Word' of the Year in 2015.

Perhaps you're yet to be convinced, but however you feel about them personally, many brands report emojis increasing engagement on shared content—so your program's content creators shouldn't be afraid of using them.

Though many of your advocates will prefer to keep their social media profiles strictly professional, you might be surprised by just how many will be more than happy to share content that includes emojis.

Try offering your advocates both emoji and emoji-free versions of the same content and monitor the results.

A word of warning though, don't overdo it. Use 1-2 emojis per post, and only where they contextually make sense. This adds a bit of visual interest and makes your content eye-catching in-feed, without detracting from the value your content is adding. Overusing emojis just for the sake of including them will make your posts look messy and unprofessional.

Try using emojis as bullet points, like this:

Bradley Keenan 🏃 (He/Him)
Founder & CEO of DSMN8. The Employee Influencer Platform. Grow ...
1yr · 🌐

Employee Advocacy = Employee Acquisition 🧲

Whether you like it or not...

Your company has an #EmployerBrand.

So, what's it worth to actively work on it? 🤔

 It REDUCES recruitment costs

 It attracts the RIGHT people

 And helps to RETAIN existing talent

Your employer brand is so much more than just a "nice to have".

53.

ONE SIZE DOESN'T FIT ALL: BE CONSCIOUS OF HOW SOCIAL CHANNELS VARY.

If your company's advocates are going to post on more than one social media channel, your advocacy program will need to provide different versions of content to meet different platform specs.

But it's not only character limits and image sizes that differ from platform to platform. Your program's content creators should be mindful of the 'personality' differences between social media networks, too, and tailor content with appropriate degrees of formality.

A tone that's perfect for LinkedIn may feel a bit out of place on Instagram. Consider educating advocates on best practices for each platform they'll be using.

For example, GIFs and memes work well on Facebook, but they can come across as unprofessional on LinkedIn. Long-form content is great for LinkedIn, but does anyone read a long Instagram caption? Probably not.

Employee Advocacy Content Styles For Different Platforms

 LinkedIn

- The best platform for sharing thought leadership content.
- Be professional, but don't be afraid of adding personality and emojis!
- Text-only posts are great, but switch it up with carousels, polls, and videos for more variety.

 Instagram

- Sharing photos of company away days and events is a great way to promote your company culture.
- Links don't work in Instagram captions, so direct readers to the bio link.

 TikTok

- Short, funny clips work best on TikTok. Many companies have gone viral for creating 'office banter' videos.
- Educational videos are also popular, thanks to #LearnonTikTok. Why not get your thought leaders to share their expertise?

 Facebook

- Memes and GIFs are popular on Facebook - add a bit of humor to your content!
- Find groups related to your industry and join conversations with other professionals.

54.

PROMOTE AUTHENTICITY BY ENCOURAGING STRONG POVS.

When an advocate adds their own spin to content, it will almost always outperform any post written solely by a marketing team. Do whatever you can to get your advocates to add their own perspectives when they share.

Encouraging advocates to choose post caption text options that best suit them and their network is a good stepping-stone towards them tweaking those options with touches of their own... and eventually creating their own post caption texts from scratch.

When your advocates are sharing their own thoughts, insights, expertise, and strong points of view—rather than just your corporate messaging—their audiences will begin to take more notice. The authenticity of your program will be highlighted, and your advocates will be empowered to break through as industry thought leaders.

Make awareness of the positive effects of custom content part of your onboarding procedure and ongoing training. If you decide to gamify your program, consider rewarding advocates for creating unique content.

Bradley Keenan (He/Him)
Founder & CEO of DSMN8. The Employee Influencer Platform. Grow ...
10mo ·

"Switch off your marketing brain"

Something I heard at an expo this year

Not only does it make copywriting much easier...

(Because you can write like you talk)

But it makes your writing much more relatable.

Much more authentic.

And much MUCH easier to understand

I immediately adopted this, and honestly...

I'd say I've cut my average writing time by about 50%.

And the content is performing WAYYYY better.

If you wouldn't say it on the phone.

Don't include it in your copy.

(I would SO love to credit the speaker but I simply cannot remember where I heard it)

127

55.

MIX IT UP!: WRITE MULTIPLE POST CAPTIONS WITH VARYING TONES.

Wouldn't the world be less interesting if we all sounded exactly the same? Fortunately, we have different voices and tones to suit different contexts.

Some of your advocates will be very formal on social media, whilst others will want to joke around a little. You should provide different versions of the same content to reflect your advocates' different personal brands.

For instance, an advocate with a Ph.D. in engineering may appreciate some technical content they can share about product components... whereas a marketing intern might prefer to share the same information in a more relaxed way, and with emojis.

Keep in mind, your employee advocacy program's job is to promote the voices of your advocates, not the voice of your company; and content that feels authentic to an advocate's brand is more likely to engage their audience.

The most authentic content is at least partly written by the person sharing it. We see self-written content captions generate up to three times more engagement, so it's a good idea to encourage advocates to add their own post captions and tones to content as often as possible.

The same content, in different styles:

This stuff might seem obvious...

But I still see a surprising number of branded images in my feed that incorporate cheesy stock photos.

I understand that some image styles might not be suitable for certain brands, but a lot of the stock photos I see would be considered too bland for a corporate employee handbook from the late nineties, let alone for a LinkedIn post in 2023.

If you're running an employee advocacy program, you'll know that images play an important role in generating more clicks, so it pays to take the time to get it right.

All (or most) marketers will know what I'm talking about!

When it comes to sharing links on social...

The image you choose to use could make or break your post.

If you're asking people to stop, read, and click, then you need to be prepared to take the time to create a truly engaging image.

This might sound like obvious stuff, but I still see an alarming number of cheesy stock photos in my feed from companies that operate in (what might be considered as) 'fun' industries.

There is just way too much content in people's feeds for marketers to be producing bland images that don't stand out in the feed.

- Keep your target audience in mind when selecting images

- Avoid dull, cheesy stock photos

- Use custom/branded graphics for a unique look

One to bookmark if you're in the content creation space!

56.
FOCUS ON PROFESSIONAL SOCIAL MEDIA CHANNELS.
IT'S MORE LIKELY TO BE ACCEPTED BY EMPLOYEES, *AND* REACH THE RIGHT AUDIENCE.

It's a misconception that advocacy programs expect employees to use their personal social media accounts to share company content. Most employees would see this as overstepping the boundary into their personal lives and reject the idea anyway.

In reality, most employee advocacy programs focus on professional networking, via platforms like LinkedIn. It is possible to make advocates want to utilize their personal social media accounts by using gamification—but the tone and strategies required for successful advocacy on Instagram, for example, will probably be very different from those you'd use on LinkedIn... and if you wouldn't share a piece of content on your Instagram account, don't expect anyone else to share it on theirs.

Your company might love the idea of its employees advocating on their personal social media accounts. We've

130

seen amazing examples of employee advocacy on TikTok and Instagram—the well-known Dunkin' Donuts advocacy program, for example.

But don't be fooled into thinking that advocating on personal social media accounts will work for every brand.

Yes, your advocates could share company event pictures on their Instagram profiles, but will they reach your target audience this way?

Advocacy via professional social media accounts is far more likely to be accepted by your employees, and far more likely to result in an audience that's actually interested in your company content.

IF YOU WOULDN'T SHARE A PIECE OF CONTENT ON YOUR INSTAGRAM ACCOUNT, DON'T EXPECT ANYONE ELSE TO SHARE IT ON THEIRS.

57.

USE AI TO SPEED UP CONTENT CREATION, BUT DON'T DEPEND ON IT.

AI is all the rage at the moment. From writing assistants to social media scheduling tools, AI certainly has a use case when it comes to employee advocacy.

These tools can help scale your advocacy program by speeding up the content generation process. For example, I recommend providing your advocates with 5 different titles and captions for every post. AI can create these variations quickly, providing a quick starting point for your content.

Generative AI is a powerful tool, but the key word here is tool. It should go without saying, don't share AI content without editing it first. This is particularly important for regulated industries like pharmaceuticals or finance—the last thing you want is employees sharing factually inaccurate content.

Test out these tools and use them to work smarter, but don't become dependent on them. Nothing screams 'inauthentic' more than advocates sharing AI-generated content without making it their own. Employee advocacy works not just because employees share content, but because employees share their own expertise and creativity!

AI CONTENT GUIDELINES

1 PROOFREAD AND FACT-CHECK

THE MOST IMPORTANT PART! PROOFREAD
EVERYTHING PRODUCED BY AI, AND IF FACTS ARE
USED, CHECK THEM. AI IS NOTORIOUS FOR MAKING
UP STATISTICS.

2 USE IT AS AN ASSISTANT

PEOPLE FOLLOW YOU FOR **YOUR** CONTENT, NOT AI
CONTENT. USE IT AS AN ASSISTANT TO HELP YOU
GENERATE IDEAS OR DRAFTS, NOT AS A
REPLACEMENT CONTENT CREATOR.

3 ADD YOUR OWN PERSONALITY!

THERE'S NOTHING MORE BORING THAN GENERIC AI
CONTENT. ADD YOUR OWN TONE OF VOICE AND
PERSONALITY TO EACH POST.

58.

COMMENTS ARE ENGAGEMENT GOLD. RESPOND TO THEM!

One of the worst things your advocates can do is share content, then ignore the comments. Advocates should genuinely want to engage with their followers and connections.

Bear in mind that social media is social. It shouldn't be used simply to bombard your audience with your own content. People want to follow people, not profiles that look like bots.

Encourage your advocates to engage with content from industry thought leaders. Not only will it increase their visibility, but it will enable them to build genuine professional relationships in their area of expertise.

Don't forget that social media algorithms reward you for engagement, and comments are typically valued more highly than likes. A great way to incite discussion is by asking a question in your post, but make sure you reply to the responses, or you'll come across as rude!

SOCIAL MEDIA ALGORITHMS VALUE COMMENTS MORE THAN LIKES.

SO SHOULD YOU.

59.

USE 'EVERGREEN CONTENT'... THEN USE IT AGAIN.

Some of your program's content will be time-sensitive: topical news pieces, promotions of company events, and articles about seasonal products and services. These can only be shared until a certain date.

But 'evergreen content' is always relevant, allowing it to be shared to good effect over and over again, regardless of time.

Content costs money to create, and you'll undoubtedly want the best returns on your investments, so the more evergreen content you can give your advocates to draw from, the better. Based on our experience, about 60% of the content that companies create is evergreen.

Why not pre-prepare every new advocate's first five posts? New advocates in your sales department, for instance, could then easily communicate your products and services to their networks in a specifically structured way.

You might need a different set of five posts for each of your company's departments, but they'll only need to be written once. This content will be shared by every new advocate, regardless of when they join your program.

Creating lots of evergreen content will not only ensure your advocates always have something to share but also reduce 'fresh content pressure' on program leaders.

Categorize your program content by time sensitivity, and make plenty of evergreen content available to your advocates year-round.

THE 3 PILLARS OF EVERGREEN CONTENT:

1 INFORMATIONAL CONTENT

E.G. GUIDES ABOUT YOUR INDUSTRY.

2 INSPIRATIONAL CONTENT

E.G. CASE STUDIES, TIMELESS WISDOM.

3 EDUCATIONAL CONTENT

E.G. HOW-TO ARTICLES, SOLVING A PROBLEM.

60.

BREAK THE CHAINS: LET EMPLOYEES CREATE CONTENT.

It's particularly important that your advocacy program finds and empowers expert employees to share their strong, informed opinions—especially if your program's leaders and main content creators aren't experts in your company's field.

The authentic voices of those advocates will make for content far more likely to resonate with other experts, both inside and outside your company... and that will mean more shares! But it's not about your program leaders asking those company experts to take on frequent tasks on their behalf, of course. If your program can foster a network of expert content creators, each advocate might only need to author one or two posts a year to create a steady stream of strong point-of-view content.

Your company's expert employees are thought leaders-in-waiting. Identify them, bring them into your marketing sphere, and they might quickly become part of your advocacy program's content creation strategy. If you ask their advice about what they think should be included in the next company blog, for instance, they may even offer to write it for you.

Bradley Keenan 🎖 (He/Him)
Founder & CEO of DSMN8. The Employee Influencer Platform. Grow ...
8mo · 🌐

Employee advocacy is not (and should not look like) spam 🗑

Here's what most employee advocacy programs do wrong...

They upload their content to their platform.

Which their employees then share at the same time.

With the same caption.

The same image.

Same title.

Everything identical.

Identical sharing at scale.

Employee advocacy shouldn't be like this 🙈

61.

WORK IN HARMONY: ALIGN CONTENT WITH MARKETING CAMPAIGNS.

Aligning your advocacy campaigns to work with your marketing campaigns will naturally bolster the impacts of both—as long as the messaging matches up.

Of course, the tone and language used by your employee advocates shouldn't sound like marketing speak, it needs to be authentic.

There's no point in trying to get marketing and employee advocacy to work together if they're focusing on entirely different areas of your business and giving different messaging. So wherever possible, the two should be thematically and strategically aligned.

For example, if your company page is focused on Pride in June for employer branding purposes, you might ask your advocates to share their own content about Pride festivals and the inclusivity of your company.

Prospective clients will follow not only your company on social media but also your employee advocates. So, you'll need company and advocate messages to complement, rather than contradict each other.

THE TONE AND LANGUAGE USED BY YOUR EMPLOYEE ADVOCATES SHOULDN'T SOUND LIKE MARKETING SPEAK, IT NEEDS TO BE AUTHENTIC.

62.

SHOWCASE EXPERTISE BY SHARING THIRD-PARTY CONTENT.

If you want your employee advocacy program to be successful, don't make the mistake of thinking of it as a direct marketing tool to be filled with company-centric content.

Instead, think of it as a medium through which your employees can share content to position themselves as experts... which, in turn, will promote your company indirectly.

Your program should create and curate plenty of content based on third-party and other industry news. This will enable your advocates to build trust with their audiences by highlighting the breadth of their expertise, not just advertising your company, but educating by sharing useful information and industry insights.

Whilst the majority of your program's content will be created by your company, there will likely be plenty of content produced externally that supports your company goals. For example, sharing content created by clients wouldn't just be good for your program: it can also deepen client relationships. Imagine your advocates celebrating the success of one of your top clients, and how much goodwill that would generate!

I recommend that around 30% of the content your program provides to your advocates should be produced externally.

Bradley Keenan 🦋 (He/Him)
Founder & CEO of DSMN8. The Employee Influencer Platform. Grow ...
1yr · 🌐

TUESDAY TIP .

Content is more likely to be shared by your employees when it's not overly sales or promotional.

Instead, focus on:

-Expertise
-Learnings
-Lessons
-Making potential customers smarter

63.
PERFECTION IS THE ENEMY OF SOCIAL MEDIA. CONSISTENCY IS KEY.

To easily scale your employee advocacy program, your program's leaders will need to know what kind of content resonates most with your advocates. The easiest way to find out is by consistently producing different types of content quickly, and monitoring how each type performs.

Perhaps your advocates will prefer long-form content, or perhaps shorter, snappier posts. The types, forms, and subjects they like most will be evident from the sharing stats. If they like something, they'll share it, and if they don't... perhaps that'll be content best avoided in future.

The most important thing for your content creators to focus on is that consistency almost always beats perfection.

It's a strange paradox as it often seems the larger a marketing team is, the more time they spend on content and yet the less content they actually produce...

In many cases, company creative leaders are so afraid of the possible consequences of a bad post that it paralyzes them. They feel that only perfection will do—and yet, when they're finally happy enough with a piece of content to launch it, it might still get no traction, making them feel that all the editing was a big waste of time.

Too many cooks spoil the employee advocacy broth. When producing regular content, avoid complicated sign-offs. Trust your creative team to get the work done.

Of course, in regulated industries, it's very important that content is checked to make sure it's completely accurate— but that's an exception to the general rule.

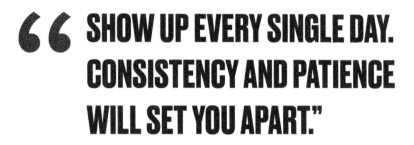

" SHOW UP EVERY SINGLE DAY. CONSISTENCY AND PATIENCE WILL SET YOU APART."

GARY VAYNERCHUK, AMERICAN ENTREPRENEUR, AUTHOR, SPEAKER, AND INTERNET PERSONALITY.

64.
NEVER SCRAPE THE BARREL: REGULARLY UPDATE YOUR MEDIA LIBRARY.

Stock images suck. There's nothing worse than cheesy pictures of random people in suits shaking hands. For your employee advocacy program to get flying, it'll need a strong media library full of relatable and appealing images.

However, your social media manager can't be everywhere at once to take photos of everything. So wherever possible, images should be gathered directly from employees. Away day team photos, new starter's first day photos... your program should find as much authentic image content as possible and categorize it based on key objectives.

Of course, images that don't exist can't be found and used, so your program should encourage your employees to take more photos. For instance, awarding a prize for the best company away day picture would be an inexpensive way to gain access to a whole lot of images... perhaps more images than your program might be able to use. These images may be useful for showcasing your company culture on your internal communications platform, as well as for social media posts.

Photos taken by your employees will be especially useful for talent acquisition. Your advocates' posts about upcoming employment opportunities will be far more effective if supported by authentic images.

 Bradley Keenan 🏃 (He/Him)
Founder & CEO of DSMN8. The Employee Influencer Platform. Grow yo...
17h · 🌐

Is it time to update your media library?

When it comes to sharing links on social...

The image you choose to use could make or break your post.

If you're asking people to stop, read, and click, then you need to be prepared to take the time to create a truly engaging image.

This might sound like obvious stuff, but I still see an alarming number of cheesy stock photos in my feed from companies that operate in (what might be considered) "fun" industries.

There is just way too much content in people's feeds for marketers to be producing bland images that don't stand out in the feed.

◈ Keep your target audience in mind when selecting images

◈ Avoid dull, cheesy stock photos

◈ Use custom/branded graphics for a unique look

◈ Lean into employee-generated content

That last one is often overlooked.

Your audiences want to see the people behind the logo.

Small changes can make a huge difference.

65.

PROVIDE HYPER-RELEVANT CONTENT FOR EACH EMPLOYEE: SET UP 'MICRO-PROGRAMS' BY DEPARTMENT OR GEOGRAPHY.

Divide your program into micro-programs by department or geography, and appoint a team leader in charge of content curation for each one. This will not only reduce the workload for your advocacy program leader, it will also allow you to tap into department-specific or local knowledge. This makes each team's shared content more relevant to their audience.

As your program grows, it will naturally pull in advocates from more areas of your business—and each area will have its own agenda. Swimming with this current can make it much easier to scale your program, so consider reaching out to HR and Sales teams, and any other departments that will see value in curating their own content.

You might also consider onboarding advocates purely for their willingness to create and curate content. Passionate advocates with creative flair can be great assets to your program, whether they're micro-program leaders or not.

Delegating at least some of your program's content creation and curation will allow your program leaders to focus on program management and policy instead—tasks that cannot be delegated. Plus, it ensures that the content provided is relevant to each employee.

4 WAYS TO SEGMENT YOUR MICRO-PROGRAMS:

1 REGION (E.G. USA, CANADA, EUROPE)

2 LANGUAGE (E.G. ENGLISH, SPANISH)

3 DEPARTMENT (E.G. SALES, HR, MARKETING)

4 SENIORITY (E.G. SALES EXECS, C-SUITE)

66.

NEED A QUICK ENGAGEMENT BOOST? SHARE COMPANY INSIGHTS.

Not every piece of content for your employee advocates needs to be created by marketing. Your organization already has lots of content you may not have thought to share.

Some of the best-performing content that I see in employee advocacy programs often includes material sharing business insights.

This could be financial reports to the stock market, announcements of new Senior Executive hires, or acquisitions your company has made.

Utilize the news page of your website to find the latest company information and press releases that can be shared by your employees.

Sometimes you need a quick win for engagement, and sharing these types of content provides exactly that.

Bradley Keenan 🎙 (He/Him)
Founder & CEO of DSMN8. The Employee Influencer Platform. Grow yo...
1mo · 🌐

Big Announcement - The wolf pack is complete

Many of you will already know that we are a self-funded business. What does this mean? Well, it means many things, but one of the most obvious is that we have no outside investors. While our competitors have given away large chunks of their businesses to VC firms, we have remained 100% in control of ours. However, this means we can only do things when we can afford to. The upside is that we are profitable and debt free. This has recently become 'fashionable', but something we have done since day one.

Simply put. No VCs = total control over our journey.

As we have grown over the last five years from just Ryan Marsh, Haris Basic and me, I have slowly handed over leadership responsibility for the various divisions to people far more capable than me. I consider myself average at most things in business, but I am great at hiring people better than me (Maybe it's too easy, haha).

This started when Jody Leon 🍃 joined the business four years ago to lead marketing. Then in 2021, James Keenan joined and took hold of the DSMN8 product. So that leaves our revenue function. As someone who has worked in business development all my life, this was naturally the last area for me to relinquish control over. However, a few months back, I accepted that to take DSMN8 into the next growth phase (and remaining self-funded), I needed a true revenue leader to join the team.

After only a few Zoom calls, I was 99% sure he was the missing part of the DSMN8 leadership team. So, to check that final 1%, I decided to jump on a flight to check that this guy was the real deal, and luckily for DSMN8 he is. Neal not only shares our core values, but he also believes in our vision for the future of the employee advocacy category.

DSMN8 has always focused on sustainable YOY growth, and we achieved this during Covid, and our growth remains consistent this year. How? It's simple. We don't hire to fill seats. We wait and focus on finding genuine diamonds (This is why we have 0% voluntary staff churn, five stars on Glassdoor and no internal politics). Customers feel this, even in things as simple as not having their account managers and support teams change every month.

This may sound like a humble brag, and in a way, it is. But in reality, do I know what I am doing? Nope, not really. While my last business had a successful exit and allowed me to fund DSMN8, this business is already way beyond my previous company in headcount, market position, revenue and pretty much any other measurable metric. So it's critical that I build a leadership team that is far more capable than me in their areas of expertise, and this could not be more true than having Neal join DSMN8.

Welcome to DSMN8 - The Employee Influence Platform Neal Stanborough

The journey is only just getting started!

67.
"GOT ANY IDEAS?": ENCOURAGE ADVOCATES TO SUGGEST CONTENT.

Your company doesn't need to create all of its employee advocacy content. Much of it can be sourced from industry news sites, for example.

But finding that content could be a job in its own right. Alleviate that workload by empowering your advocates to make content suggestions.

Using your advocates as content scouts may have other benefits, too. Your program leaders are more likely to have marketing, HR, or personal branding backgrounds than relevant product/service expertise.

Your advocates finding an article interesting enough to share may be a better indicator of whether it will resonate with their networks than advocacy program leaders' opinions.

Plan a workflow to allow your advocates to suggest content for you to curate. Creating a message channel for your program will enable advocates to send in content links and give feedback.

Make sure your program leaders encourage this by crediting and congratulating advocates for their content suggestions and creativity.

Here's a trending topic in our industry, perhaps our thought leaders could comment on the news?

This article would be great to share with our engineering team's networks!

Here's a TED talk that would resonate with our ICP, maybe advocates could share it?

68.

"NO HABLO INGLES!": MAKE ADVOCACY LANGUAGE-FRIENDLY.

If you're looking to roll out your employee advocacy program globally, you'll need to remove language barriers.

It's possible you're a multilingual genius who speaks every language needed to run your program internationally (and has the time on your hands to do so). Realistically, most companies will need to appoint local team leaders, fluent in the languages of their parent companies and their own regions, to create micro versions of their employee advocacy programs (as mentioned in chapter 67).

One of the most engaged geographies for employee advocacy is Latin America, where most content is shared in Portuguese. Be mindful that if your social post captions are going to be in Portuguese, your content also needs to be in Portuguese. It would be very frustrating for a reader to assume that they're going to be able to read content, only to click on it and be presented with a language that they don't understand.

Given that, on the whole, most social media content is written in English, if you are able to provide content in local languages, it will stand out and get more engagement from those geographies.

This also helps with advocate adoption. Some employees won't speak English, so by only providing your content in English, you are limiting the number of people that can join and take advantage of your program.

Providing content in different languages also enables you to regionalize your content. If you sell different products or services to different markets, you can serve selected content for your advocates to share. I have said it before, but providing the "right content to the right people" will help boost social media engagement.

SOME EMPLOYEES WON'T SPEAK ENGLISH, SO BY ONLY PROVIDING YOUR CONTENT IN ENGLISH, YOU ARE LIMITING THE NUMBER OF PEOPLE THAT CAN JOIN AND TAKE ADVANTAGE OF YOUR PROGRAM.

69.

GAMIFICATION AND PRIZES ARE GREAT! JUST DON'T RELY ON THEM.

Gamification works! But sometimes it works too well.

It's easy to see rewards and prizes as a great shortcut to creating a culture that celebrates employee advocacy. The problem is, it can also undermine the core principle of creating a successful program.

Yes, it's great to reward people for doing good work. But doing so risks changing your advocacy program from an initiative to a game—one in which advocates believe they will be rewarded every time they share content.

That's not only a very expensive game, but also one that encourages employees to share content more than they naturally would, negatively impacting your program's overall performance. You don't want people to share content in droves just for the sake of it, you want them to provide real value to audiences.

Beware: if people are sharing only for prizes, employee activity may dry up as soon as the prize budget does. So use prizes intermittently.

If a weekly prize becomes the norm, prizes will lose their novelty. Instead, use prizes to highlight specific campaigns, or at certain times of the year. That way, employees won't take them for granted. Not knowing when the next competition might begin may also spur more of your employees to get involved.

100 ACTIVE AMBASSADORS USING YOUR PROGRAM WELL IS FAR MORE PRODUCTIVE THAN 10,000 USING IT JUST TO GET PRIZES.

Gamification is a great trigger for engagement, but it should never be allowed to become the main reason employees want to advocate for your company.

70.
PUT A FACE TO YOUR BRAND WITH VIDEO CONTENT.

It's no secret that video content has dominated social media in the past few years.

With the rise of short-form vertical videos thanks to TikTok, Instagram Reels, and YouTube Shorts, it's clear that this isn't a short-lived trend.

Video content helps put a face to your company, increasing trust with your audience. It's also more engaging than a text-only post, and eye-catching in the feed. Social media algorithms reward video content too, so getting on board can help your company and advocates grow quicker.

There's no need to reinvent the wheel. To get started, simply repurpose some of your written content into video form. If you stick to the script verbatim, you can also use the original text for closed captions, increasing accessibility. Don't worry about high quality video production, as long as you can be seen and heard clearly, it's good to go.

This isn't about changing your content strategy from text to video, it's about creating variation in the types of content your advocates can share.

Don't make this exclusive to marketing either. Share the idea with leadership and top advocates, they might want to create videos of their own!

Bradley Keenan 🐾 (He/Him)
Founder & CEO of DSMN8. The Employee Influencer Platform ...
1mo · 🌐

I remember getting excited about producing 10 podcast episodes.

Now I'm announcing the launch of the 2nd season.

Very happy to say that the 1st episode of our podcast's 2nd season is now live

A while back, I asked Lewis Gray to co-host the podcast with me, and we've also totally re-vamped the show with a brand new look and format.

Season 2 kicks off with us tackling a highly debated topic within the employee advocacy space: what are the biggest enemies of employee advocacy success?

By "enemies" we mean potential problems or roadblocks that could prevent your program from reaching its full potential.

We covered everything from dodgy outdated social media policies to over-involved internal communications teams (which will make more sense post-listen!).

We are super eager to get some feedback on this, so please do feel free to drop me a DM if you have any initial thoughts/feedback

New episodes will be released every Wednesday.

Enjoy!

#EmployeeAdvocacy #DigitalMarketing #SocialSelling #EmployerBranding #PersonalBranding

[Podcast] Season 2 Premiere: The 3 Enemies Of Employee Advocacy | DSMN8

71.
WANT AN ENGAGEMENT BOOST? TAG OTHERS!

Your employee advocacy program's content creators should tag your company's advocates and employees in their content whenever relevant and appropriate.

It won't matter whether it's a shout-out to thank or congratulate a team on their good work, or a way to ask for opinions from people the piece is relevant to—tagging people is an effective and natural way to drive engagement.

Sharing a third-party article? Tag the publication and the author/journalist. They'll be grateful for the visibility and may re-share your post too.

Your content creators shouldn't tag at random or by the hundred, though. It's poor online etiquette, which will be bound to result in negative feedback.

Bradley Keenan 🎣 (He/Him) ● ● ●
Founder & CEO of DSMN8. The Employee Influencer Platform. ...
4mo · 🌐

5 Reasons that salespeople should post on LinkedIn.

Reason 1 - When I think of LinkedIn ads, I think of Justin Rowe

Reason 2 - When I think of using the telephone as a sales tool, I think of Ryan Reisert and Gerry Hill 🚀

Reason 3 - When I think of email sequences, I think of Steve Schmidt

Reason 4 - When I think about ABM, I think of 🌐 Paul Sullivan

Reason 5 - When I think of email deliverability, I think of Jesse Ouellette

I guess these are all the same reasons.

Be the person people think about when they need what you sell.

161

72.
#OVERDOING IT: DON'T OVERUSE HASHTAGS.

Using hashtags is a great way to tap into the social media feeds of users following particular topics.

When Chris Messina invented the hashtag in 2007, it was considered too nerdy for widespread use. These days, hashtags are used all over social media—but often not very sensibly.

Using up to three hashtags inside body content is great... but many users seem to believe that plastering relevant (or even irrelevant) hashtags all over their content, or in a block at the end of a post, will boost their engagement. Perhaps that worked for a short spell in 2008, but it certainly doesn't work now. Using more than five hashtags on LinkedIn makes your content look like spam, actually reducing the number of users it gets seen by.

An accessible list of hashtags relevant to your company and/or used by your marketing team should help your advocates choose the right ones and not misuse them. Creating a specific, individual hashtag to be used only by your advocates is also a good idea. It will make your advocates' posts more easily searchable, and demarcate members of your employee advocacy program from other social media users.

3 TYPES OF HASHTAGS TO USE:

1 YOUR BRANDED HASHTAG

E.G. #COMPANY #COMPANYTEAM
#LIFEATCOMPANY

2 INDUSTRY HASHTAGS

E.G. #MARKETING #SOCIALMEDIA #SALES
#EMPLOYERBRANDING

3 CONTENT TOPIC HASHTAGS

E.G. #MARKETINGSTRATEGY #SOCIALSELLING
#COMPANYCULTURE #WOMENINTECH

73.
YOU KNOW WHO LOVES CLICKBAIT? NOBODY. AVOID!

Don't be tempted to drive results at the expense of your employee advocacy program's credibility.

Using shock-tactic headlines—or any other form of clickbait—is a big mistake.

One of your program's most important assets will be the trust of your advocates' connections. If those connections feel they've been lied to or tricked into opening content, that trust will be eroded—and the connections may well make their feelings about that clear with negative comments. Or worst-case scenario, they decide to never open your content again.

Your program's direct results shouldn't be measured by how many social media users read the content your advocates post, but by how many readers take action. Whether that action is downloading more of your content or booking a demo session with one of your salespeople, they won't take it if they don't trust your company.

MAKE SURE YOUR ADVOCATES KNOW THAT BUILDING *TRUST* IS THE GOAL,

NOT SIMPLY GENERATING VIEWS & CLICKS IN ANY WAY POSSIBLE.

LEVEL 5:

EXECUTIVE INFLUENCE

74.
EMPOWER YOUR THOUGHT LEADERS (THE MVPS!).

Industry experts are the MVPs (most valuable players) of any employee advocacy program. Whatever your industry is, you'll have some experts on your team, like your engineers, scientists, or your senior leaders.

These people have a unique view of what is going on in your industry, making them the perfect candidates for becoming thought leaders.

Whether it's commentary on industry trends or sharing their latest research, your experts will create content that adds value to their audience. Their expertise may be niche, but niche is the way to build a focused audience.

Get your experts on board and they'll also be likely to suggest valuable content that other advocates can share. Empower them to share their insights, and you'll reap the rewards.

Want to help your employees become thought leaders? Share my checklist with them.

3 STEPS TO BECOMING A THOUGHT LEADER:

1. Establish Credibility

- Optimize your LinkedIn profile.
- Highlight your qualifications, experience & skills. Why should people trust you?
- Connect with authoritative people in your industry. Leave insightful comments.

2. Create Content That Showcases Your Expertise

- Educate & Inspire! Always add value.
- Keep up with industry news, share latest research and add your opinion.
- Mix up your content: blog posts, research papers, videos, podcasts.

3. Share Your Insights on Social Media

- Remember that social media is social! Engage with your followers, and ask for their opinion.
- Consistency is key! You're not going to become a thought leader in a week.

75.
SENIOR LEADERSHIP PARTICIPATION = WINNING.

Your company's senior leaders will naturally have more extensive and valuable social media connections than somebody who has just started in their career.

Such leaders have nurtured their careers over many years and will be connected to more prospective clients and potential hires—and perhaps even to members of the press.

Onboarding senior leaders has its challenges though, particularly when trying to drive social media usage. Many of them will be (to put it politely) 'non-digital-natives'. They are more likely to have forgotten their LinkedIn password than to be posting daily.

Nonetheless, they are your thought leaders, so they should be active on social—talking about the company and industry news... and perhaps even employee advocacy.

Your company's senior leaders have a vested interest in the business, so it shouldn't be a hard sell to activate them, and doing so is a critical step to achieving a scaled-out employee advocacy program.

The simple reason for this is that employees will follow the example set by their senior leadership. So leaders are not only great advocates for sharing content, but they can also become role models for employees.

They tend to be a competitive crowd, too. Create a social media leaderboard to pit them against each other, and watch their efforts skyrocket. They will all want to be top of the leaderboard—even if it's just for bragging rights.

YOUR COMPANY'S SENIOR LEADERS HAVE A VESTED INTEREST IN THE BUSINESS, SO IT SHOULDN'T BE A HARD SELL TO ACTIVATE THEM, AND DOING SO IS A CRITICAL STEP TO ACHIEVING A SCALED-OUT EMPLOYEE ADVOCACY PROGRAM.

76.

IF YOUR CEO ISN'T INVOLVED, MAKE IT HAPPEN!

Of the 200,000+ CEOs in the US, how many can you actually name? Perhaps Elon Musk, Bill Gates, Mark Cuban...? And what do those three CEOs have in common? They're all ubiquitous on social media.

Despite ever-increasing evidence that having a social media-active CEO helps a company close deals, attract and retain talent, and improve internal communications, many CEOs remain silent. Perhaps the potential consequences of a social media mistake feel bigger than the immediate upsides of being active.

No, not every CEO needs to be a kickass content creator. But what message will it send to your company's employees if even your CEO doesn't bother to participate? You'll need them to be an active part of your program, setting the tone for the rest of your organization, and giving permission for employees to advocate. After all, if the CEO isn't sharing, why would they?

As the figurehead of your organization, your CEO should be your company's most important advocate—its thought leader. They won't need to post every day (although it'd be great if they did), but they will need to actively increase your company's visibility.

" **THE ULTIMATE GIFT, IN OUR DIGITAL AGE, IS A CEO WHO HAS THE STORYTELLING TALENT TO CAPTURE THE IMAGINATION OF THE MARKETS WHILE SURROUNDING THEMSELVES WITH PEOPLE WHO CAN SHOW INCREMENTAL PROGRESS AGAINST THAT VISION EACH DAY."**

SCOTT GALLOWAY, AUTHOR OF *THE FOUR: THE HIDDEN DNA OF AMAZON, APPLE, FACEBOOK, AND GOOGLE.*

77.

BOOST SENIOR LEADERSHIP POSTS: THEIR CONTENT IS STRATEGICALLY IMPORTANT.

It's likely that some of your employees will want to be involved in your advocacy program, but won't feel comfortable posting themselves. That's OK. There will be scope for them to help your program in other ways.

For example, you could ask them to focus on engaging with the posts of your senior leadership and strategically important advocates. These are the people in your organization who have the most expertise and the most valuable audiences.

We ran a test at DSMN8 to compare employee social media posts that were boosted via co-workers with those that were not. The results were clear. Where we had at least 10 interactions from co-workers (reactions or comments), the posts achieved a 3.8X greater reach. The more people engaged, the more reach the content had.

Giving senior leadership posts early engagement momentum boosts them up the algorithm rankings and helps drive further growth.

YOUR PROGRAM LEADERS
SHOULD EMBRACE THE IDEA
THAT EVERY ADVOCATE CAN
BE USEFUL, EVEN THE ONES
WHO AREN'T COMFORTABLE
WITH SHARING ORIGINAL
CONTENT YET.

LEVEL 6:

MAINTAINING MOMENTUM

78.
EYES ON THE PRIZE: REGULARLY COMMUNICATE THE PROGRAM'S NORTH STAR.

Your company's advocates will need regular reminders of your program's goals in order to make sure they're all aligned and maintaining the right mindset.

They must never be allowed to forget why the program was started and why they're participating in it.

Regular reminders will also keep the importance of the program firmly in C-suite-level executives' minds— something that'll be useful when it comes to asking for its budget to be maintained.

Don't let the energy generated by the work put into your program's launch slip away—it'll be easier to maintain those levels of attention, enthusiasm, and focus than win them back.

" WHEN PEOPLE ARE FINANCIALLY INVESTED, THEY WANT A RETURN. WHEN PEOPLE ARE EMOTIONALLY INVESTED, THEY WANT TO CONTRIBUTE."

SIMON SINEK, AUTHOR AND MOTIVATIONAL SPEAKER.

79.
GONE BUT NOT FORGOTTEN: RE-ENGAGE DORMANT ADVOCATES.

Have you ever returned to work after a holiday and found that to begin with, you could barely remember your own job?

Workplace disengagement and re-engagement is usually a completely natural process, but may be more of an impactful issue for your employee advocacy program. As advocacy is likely to be a secondary activity for your employees, they may not re-engage with it quite as naturally as with their other tasks.

Your program's leaders should aim to minimize disengagement through regular communication. They could, for example, send monthly emails to all advocates to share program results and mention top users, standout shares, and favorite pieces of content.

But even with regular communication to keep your program at the front of advocates' minds, some may disengage and become dormant. Your program leaders will need to track those advocates and create processes to re-engage them. In many cases, a gentle email reminder will be enough, but other advocates may need more training to bring them back into the fold.

3 WAYS TO RE-ENGAGE DORMANT ADVOCATES

1 SEND AN UPDATE

THIS COULD BE A SIMPLE 'HERE'S WHAT YOU MISSED' EMAIL, SHARING SOME OF YOUR BEST RECENT CONTENT.

2 ASK FOR PROGRAM FEEDBACK

FIND OUT IF THERE'S A REASON THEY LOST INTEREST. IS THE CONTENT SUITABLE? DO THEY FEEL CONFIDENT ON SOCIAL MEDIA?

3 OFFER ADDITIONAL TRAINING

HELP WHEREVER POSSIBLE. IF THEY FEEL UNSURE ABOUT CREATING CONTENT, DON'T KNOW HOW TO BUILD AN AUDIENCE, OR NEED SOME REMINDERS, OFFER TRAINING!

80.
COMPETITION GENERATES ACTIVITY: CREATE COMPETITIVE LEADERBOARDS.

Gamification and leaderboards are not necessarily the same thing. When we think about gamification, it is more about providing rewards for activity. Leaderboards, on the other hand, are more about friendly competition without the incentives.

Leaderboards are a very simple and effective way of creating a competitive environment. People will want to participate for the value of being seen as more effective at the task of being active on social. This is especially true when it comes to salespeople and senior leadership.

You can create a leaderboard for the entire organization, but sometimes it's more effective to create leaderboards by department or location. This way, the people who are in the leaderboards will know the other people, driving further competition to outrank their peers.

Encouraging this competitive activity is easy. Create a champions' leaderboard for your advocates that generate the most engagement in a week or month, and highlight who is leading the way each week. Let your advocates' competitive nature kick in!

SOCIAL MEDIA LEADERBOARD

 Jon Smith **20,342** points

 Ann David **16,783** points

 Emma Jones **15,009** points

4. **Will Taylor** **14,900** points

5. **James Brown** **12,876** points

81.

TREAT YOUR ADVOCATES LIKE CLIENTS: YOUR GOAL IS TO HELP THEM BECOME THOUGHT LEADERS.

Your employee advocacy program should aim to help your advocates position themselves as thought leaders. One of the best ways you can do that is by providing lots of educational content to share.

Yes, you want your program to increase sales. But if all your content is focused on selling, it won't be a functional program that increases the reach of any of your content, whatever that content might be.

Your program's clients are not your company's customers. Your program's clients are your company's advocates. Your task is not to treat employees as digital billboards, but to help them build trust within their social media networks. This will both reinforce the value of their participation and reflect positively upon your company's brand.

By providing your advocates with content their connections find useful, your program will help grow their networks in the right way. Then, when your advocates do share content designed to promote your brand, they'll be sharing it with a bigger, better, more trusting network that's more likely to engage.

" BY AUTOMATING THE SHARING OF BOTH OUR OWN CONTENT AND INTERESTING AND RELEVANT EXTERNAL CONTENT, EMPLOYEE ADVOCACY HAS HELPED DRIVE ENGAGEMENT AND CONVERSATIONS WHILE BUILDING OUR BRANDS, AND EMPOWERING OUR EMPLOYEES TO BECOME THOUGHT-LEADERS IN THE ECOSYSTEMS THEY RECRUIT FOR."

KASHIF NAQSHBANDI, CHIEF MARKETING OFFICER, FRANK RECRUITMENT GROUP*.

* FRANK RECRUITMENT GROUP IS A GLOBAL LEADER IN STAFFING FOR IT PROFESSIONALS.

82.
IT'S A TWO-WAY STREET: DON'T 'USE' YOUR ADVOCATES.

It's no secret that when you launch an employee advocacy program, the reason you're doing it is to get more content visibility, and consequently reach your business goals.

That said, it's really important that you don't simply use your advocates as a marketing channel. This should be considered a secondary benefit.

The primary benefit is positioning your employees as experts, through sharing content on social media.

Growing their networks and building personal brands can result in opportunities like public speaking, getting invited to events, or being interviewed on a podcast. This will get their name out there and they'll start becoming known as a person of influence, an industry expert, and a thought leader.

Those in marketing, sales, recruitment, or HR, will see even more benefits from becoming an employee advocate. It literally helps them do their jobs better.

Marketers want their content to be seen.

Sales reps want to build relationships with prospects and clients.

Recruiters and HR want to showcase company culture and reach the best talent.

Growing and maintaining a social media presence is the best way to do that.

Don't just list the benefits, provide training and resources to help them along the way. The increased marketing reach for your company will come as a result of adding huge value to your employees.

Bradley Keenan 🦓 (He/Him)
Founder & CEO of DSMN8. The Employee Influencer Platform. Grow ...
1yr · 🌐

There are 3 secrets every successful social media team knows about employee advocacy...

That newbies don't... Want to know them? Here they are...

Successful: Champions employee benefits.
Newbies: Champions company benefits.

Successful: Segment content so that it's hyper-relevant to the employee.
Newbies: Has no segmentation for their content.

Successful: Leverages executive influence.
Newbies: Fails to utilise senior leadership to lead by example.

So, remember...

As a phase 1, employees should be motivated to participate.

AND have content that is relevant to THEIR interests.

Give your employee advocacy efforts the time they deserve to guarantee success.

83.
"YOU'RE KILLING IT!": ACKNOWLEDGE ADVOCATE SUCCESS.

Although most employers realize their workforces need encouragement to keep up the good work, it can be more easily forgotten in the digital world.

When building an employee advocacy program, it is essential to include a 'thank you' process. We all like to receive positive affirmation, as it's evidence of our actions making a difference, but it's all too easy for a busy program leader to leave this simple but effective task undone.

You're asking people to go beyond their day-to-day role, so you must take time to thank people for participating— especially those who have gone above and beyond the call of duty.

You might achieve that with something as simple as a monthly email thanking active participants and giving shoutouts to specific standout advocates.

TAKE SHOWING YOUR APPRECIATION TO THE NEXT LEVEL BY PRE-WRITING AN EMAIL FOR YOUR CEO TO SEND OUT COMPANY-WIDE.

WHEN EMPLOYEES SEE THE CEO TAKES NOTE OF WHO IS PARTICIPATING IN THE PROGRAM, YOU WILL HAVE A QUEUE OF NEW RECRUITS AT YOUR DOOR.

84.
SEND KUDOS TO RANDOM ADVOCATES.

Acknowledging the efforts of advocates who perform extraordinarily well is a no-brainer, but do not fall into the trap of only recognizing those whose activity has generated big results.

Have you ever done something as unexceptional as holding a door open for somebody, only for them to breeze past without thanking you? That's how advocates for your business feel when they join your advocacy program but never receive feedback. Sure, they might not be setting the world alight, but as you've seen in the previous chapters, every contribution is valuable to your program's success.

Genuine, heartfelt, positive feedback has a nurturing and encouraging effect on those who receive it, whether they're 5 or 65. Its importance in the workplace should never be underestimated.

Your program leaders should give regular feedback to your company's entire advocacy network. It shouldn't be restricted to advocates who are topping the performance tables.

Reaching out to random advocates and those new to your program with an individual 'well done, and thanks for being part of this' message can really help your program keep rolling at full speed. You never know; that little pat on the back might give them a confidence boost that sends their participation soaring.

NURTURE YOUR ADVOCATES.

EVEN IF THEY'RE NOT TOP PERFORMERS, MAKE SURE EVERY ADVOCATE KNOWS THAT THEIR EFFORTS ARE APPRECIATED.

85.
SHOUT IT FROM THE ROOFTOPS!: CELEBRATE THE WINS.

Celebrate the wins, but not just among your advocates. Maintaining leadership buy-in is key for continued support, so make sure to shout about your program's successes throughout your organization.

Many of your colleagues in other business units might not know what employee advocacy is, or how it helps you reach business goals.

Showcasing the results goes a long way in gaining support and selling the concept to other departments in your company.

Do this well (and often), to drive interest and advocate uptake. This will help your entire program grow.

Plus, if advocates know you're praising them to senior management, they'll be more likely to sustain their efforts!

HOW TO MAINTAIN LEADERSHIP BUY-IN:

CELEBRATE THE WINS. SHOW THEM THE RESULTS THAT ADVOCACY IS DRIVING. PRAISE YOUR ADVOCATES, NOT JUST AMONG THE ADVOCACY TEAM, BUT WITH LEADERSHIP TOO.

86.
UNLOCK THE POWER OF POSITIVE HABITS.

How do you make something stick?

Just like checking your emails, engaging on social media should become part of your advocates' daily work routine. Sharing content every day might be a bit much, especially for time-poor executives, but building in just 15 minutes a day to engage on LinkedIn should be achievable for everyone.

Make sure your advocates are aware that you expect this to become routine for them, not just a once-in-a-while activity. Communicate that growing a social media presence is all about two things: content and consistency. Don't forget the consistency part!

A great way to build the advocacy habit is by following the 'habit stacking' method[4]. For example, after you check and respond to your emails in the morning, do the same on LinkedIn. Reply to any comments you've received, engage with your colleagues' content, and leave comments on interesting posts you see on the feed. The goal here is to make advocacy become second nature.

---

[4] Read Atomic Habits by James Clear to learn more about the habit stacking method.

THE GOAL IS TO MAKE ADVOCACY BECOME SECOND NATURE.

87.
VALIDATE!: RECOGNIZE AND ENGAGE WITH EMPLOYEES ON SOCIAL MEDIA.

Posting on social media and getting zero engagement in return can be a real confidence killer for new advocates. Your program leaders should engage with posts from advocates, by giving a like or comment.

Your program's initial engagement will not only help every post get off the ground, it will also show your advocates that program leaders are aware of and appreciate every post.

If your program is going to be large, it will be easiest to manage this strategy by creating a hashtag for your advocates to include every time they post: #(yourcompanyname)social, for example. Your company's unique hashtag will allow your program's leader to find all advocate posts across all social media networks with just one search.

Public appreciation from your program's leaders will boost the confidence of your advocates, increase the reach of their posts, and also highlight the benefits of advocacy to non-advocate employees.

ONE OF THE BIGGEST FEARS
EMPLOYEES HAVE AROUND
POSTING ON SOCIAL MEDIA?

GETTING ZERO ENGAGEMENT.

THE SOLUTION? ENGAGE WITH ALL
YOUR ADVOCATES' CONTENT,
WHETHER THEY'RE AN INTERN OR
THE CEO. ENCOURAGE THE REST
OF YOUR TEAM TO DO THE SAME.

88.
WANT TO GENERATE BUZZ ABOUT YOUR PROGRAM? SHARE SUCCESS STORIES, NOT STATISTICS.

People remember stories. They don't remember statistics.

The reality is that the average employee doesn't care about CPCs, CPAs, or any other marketing metric that you may care about.

You need to listen to feedback from the frontline to discover the real impact of your advocacy program. It could be a simple story of a salesperson closing a deal, or a recruiter finding their next hire.

This feedback will not only help you improve your advocacy program by tailoring it to employees' needs, but sharing the stories will create buzz, encouraging more people to join.

Yes, it's great to have good statistics, but it's the stories that will win you new advocates!

THE REALITY IS THAT THE AVERAGE EMPLOYEE DOESN'T CARE ABOUT CPCS, CPAS, OR ANY OTHER MARKETING METRIC THAT YOU MAY CARE ABOUT.

89.

CREATE A SUPPORT NETWORK FOR YOUR ADVOCATES.

Now and then, your advocates might feel the need for a little guidance about what to post, best practice, or perhaps something that might seem quite trivial to those in the know.

Everyone learns at their own pace and in their own way, and sometimes the answers are only obvious when you know them.

A dedicated support network your advocates can use to ask each other (and your program leaders) questions and swap ideas will be an important part of your advocacy program. Whether it's set up as a Slack channel or part of your internal communications program won't matter much, but the process must be simple and frictionless so your advocates won't hesitate to use it.

Not every advocate will be ready to fly from day one. Give the less confident a safe space to seek help. This will also allow your program's leaders to more easily gather feedback about the program from your advocates' points of view.

YOUR ADVOCACY COMMS CHANNEL SHOULD:

1 BE A SAFE SPACE FOR ASKING QUESTIONS

MAKE IT CLEAR THAT NO QUESTION IS TOO SILLY. THIS IS A SPACE TO ASK ANYTHING FROM "CAN I POST THIS?" TO "HOW DO I SET UP CREATOR MODE ON LINKEDIN?".

2 PROVIDE TRAINING + RESOURCES

YOUR ADVOCATES WILL NEED ACCESS TO RESOURCES, INCLUDING THINGS LIKE YOUR BRAND STYLE GUIDE, LOGOS, LINKEDIN COVER IMAGE TEMPLATES, AND SOCIAL MEDIA ADVICE.

3 ENCOURAGE FEEDBACK & COLLABORATION

THIS IS A GREAT OPPORTUNITY FOR MARKETING TO GET FEEDBACK ON THEIR CONTENT, AND FOR ADVOCATES TO SHARE CONTENT SUGGESTIONS.

LEVEL 7:

THE SCORE CARD

90.

BLOW YOUR OWN MIND: TRACK TOTAL FOLLOWERS/CONNECTIONS.

Here's a powerful number: the total size of your advocates' networks. Compare this to your brand accounts' followers and the figure becomes even more impressive.

The average number of followers I see for employees on LinkedIn is around 1,180.

Multiply that by the number of advocates in your program, and your potential content reach drastically increases.

And that's not even factoring in your top performers who are likely to have more followers, like your sales team or C-Suite executives.

Let's say you have 500 advocates. 500 x 1,180 = 590,000. Your content has the potential to reach 590,000 people. Use this number as a benchmark to compare with the existing size of your company accounts.

That's the power of advocacy.

This figure will help when creating future forecasts for your program. For example, if you know that your average employee has 1,180 connections, you will be able to predict the potential reach of your content once the program has scaled to 800 or 1,000 advocates.

USE <u>MY CALCULATOR</u> TO INSTANTLY SEE YOUR POTENTIAL REACH:

91.
FOCUS ON THE BIG PICTURE: MONITOR THE MACRO RESULTS.

Monitoring employee advocacy statistics weekly is great to check incremental changes and make sure you're moving in the right direction.

But, advocacy is a long-term process.

Worrying about every share or every post creates too much micro-management.

Take a step back and look at the big picture.

What are your overall results so far? What have you achieved in a year? What could you achieve next year if you doubled the number of people in the program?

Made some changes to your content style or format?

Sometimes the results take longer than others to materialize. Keep at it, and don't hyper-focus on the minute details.

Never forget the overall goal.

Bradley Keenan 🏃 (He/Him) ..
Founder & CEO of DSMN8. The Employee Influencer Platform. Grow yo...
11h · 🌐

FOCUS ON THE BIG PICTURE.

Something I've noticed a lot of employee advocacy program managers (and marketers in general) do is hyper-focus on the details.

Monitoring incremental progress is great.

But worrying about the analytics for every single piece of social content means you'll essentially start micro-managing yourself (or your advocacy program).

Take a step back.

What are your overall results looking like? Are they moving in the right direction?

Is your content helping you reach business goals?

Don't get lost in numbers and forget why you started.

92.

KEEP A CLOSER EYE ON THE NUMBERS WITH UTM TRACKING.

Attribution. Attribution. Attribution.

Understanding how many people converted from employee advocacy content is essential for demonstrating ROI.

You need to understand where your website traffic is coming from, what content is performing best, and how it's helping you reach business goals.

Advocacy tends to have a much lower bounce rate than other traffic sources, as peer-to-peer sharing is more authentic. But once they're on your website, where are people going? Are they booking a call with your sales team? Are they opting into your email newsletter?

It's time to get familiar with Google Analytics and UTM tracking.

A UTM code is simply a bit of code you can add to the end of a URL to track clicks. It's an incredibly useful tool to understand exactly where your traffic is coming from, and it'll be automatically shown within Google Analytics.

You can track 5 different parameters with UTM codes: source, medium, campaign, term, and content.

3 WAYS TO USE UTM TRACKING FOR MONITORING EMPLOYEE ADVOCACY CONTENT PERFORMANCE:

- **Track how your advocates' content performs on different social channels.** Find out which platforms drive the most website clicks, and then compare advocate clicks vs. organic social and paid social clicks in Google Analytics.

- **Monitor content performance from different teams**, e.g. Sales, Marketing, Recruitment. Who drives the most traffic? Go deeper by creating UTM tags to identify specific users. That way you can find your top performing advocates, and see whose share led to which sale.

- **Compare clicks from different content variations on the same platform.** For example, compare LinkedIn clicks by content type: short-form vs. long-form video, carousel posts, or text-only posts.

93.
TRACK METRICS, BUT DON'T FORGET ABOUT DARK SOCIAL!

Track the engagement your advocates receive on their content, but don't forget about dark social. It's the impact you can't see on the surface.

From my own experience, I regularly have potential customers send me messages on LinkedIn asking to book a call or a platform demo, saying they've seen my content and love it. But, they've never engaged with it, never commented, or even left a like. The impact is there, but it's not always visible.

Don't forget that your content can be shared privately too, anywhere from email to WhatsApp messages. Though your advocates are sharing content publicly, the impact goes beyond what is publicly visible on social media.

Sometimes employee advocacy program managers get so caught up in tracking the 'vanity metrics', e.g. shares, likes, or followers, that they forget to consider the impact that simple visibility can have.

I get it, you need to demonstrate ROI to leadership, but part of that requires making sure leadership understands that the results of social sharing cannot always be quantified.

DARK SOCIAL = SHARES THAT DO NOT CONTAIN ANY REFERRAL INFORMATION ABOUT THE SOURCE.

IT'S THE DIFFERENCE BETWEEN SHARING CONTENT PUBLICLY ON SOCIAL MEDIA, AND SHARING IT PRIVATELY THROUGH A TEXT MESSAGE.

JUST BECAUSE YOU CAN'T TRACK IT, DOESN'T MEAN IT DOESN'T EXIST.

94.

MONITOR ADVOCACY PERFORMANCE VS. YOUR COMPANY'S SOCIALS.

Before launching your advocacy program, audit your company's social channels to see where you're currently at. Analytics to audit include content reach, average engagement rates, website clicks... you get the idea.

Establish the benchmark for the results you currently achieve from social media. Later on, this data will be incredibly useful to compare with the results from your advocacy program.

Having sight of these benchmarks before launching your advocacy program gives you the opportunity to demonstrate the impact of advocacy in a clear way to your leadership team, to maintain interest and support for the program as it grows.

You're likely to see that your advocates drive more results and get more reach on social media than your brand accounts do, even though they probably have fewer followers than your company accounts.

There are several reasons for this:

1 PEOPLE TRUST PEOPLE

WE ARE ALL NATURALLY MORE INCLINED TO ENGAGE WITH PEOPLE ON SOCIAL MEDIA OVER BRANDS. THEIR CONTENT WILL COME ACROSS AS MORE TRUSTWORTHY THAN THE SAME CONTENT POSTED BY YOUR BRAND ACCOUNTS.

2 ALGORITHMS

IT'S NO SECRET THAT SOCIAL MEDIA ALGORITHMS TEND TO PROMOTE CONTENT BY PEOPLE ABOVE BRAND PAGES. THINK ABOUT IT: THEIR BUSINESS MODEL RELIES ON ADVERTISING!

3 THE HUMAN TOUCH

THE CONTENT YOUR ADVOCATES POST IS MORE LIKELY TO INCITE DISCUSSION IN THE COMMENTS, STARTING CONVERSATIONS. ESPECIALLY IF THEY'RE SHARING THEIR OWN OPINIONS OR EXPERTISE.

95.
LOVE ROI?
TRACK EARNED MEDIA VALUE.

Every business project should create some kind of value, and it's always important to understand what that value is. When it comes to employee advocacy programs, a great way to measure value is by calculating 'earned media value.'

Dividing your existing online advertising costs—paid ads on LinkedIn or Facebook—by your current website visits per year will give you the current average advertising cost of each visit.

Now, the average active employee advocate shares 2.2 items of content per week, which will generate around 450-500 visits to their company's website per year.

Let's assume your program will have 500 advocates who keep up with that sharing average. Between them, simply by sharing content, they should generate at least 225,000 visits to your company's website per year.

Assuming a cost of $5 per click, the generation of 225,000 website visits using LinkedIn paid advertising would cost your company $1,125,000. Do you think a 500-advocate employee advocacy program will cost your company that much?

I doubt it!

In fact, a well-executed employee advocacy program should provide at least ten times the ROI of conventional social media advertising—possibly bringing your advertising purchase price down to what it might've been in the late 1990s.

As your program grows and scales throughout your organization, it'll create more and more content engagement that'll convert into more and more website traffic. That 'earned media value' figure might well get pretty big indeed, creating a compelling story inside your company.

USE MY <u>ROI CALCULATOR</u> TO INSTANTLY SEE THE IMPACT:

96.
KEEP BUILDING YOUR BUSINESS CASE... AND BE READY TO BACK IT.

It's quite possible that some of your company's C-level executives won't fully understand your employee advocacy program's value, and so won't be as supportive of it as they should be.

Because of that, it'll be important for your program's leaders to be ready and able to demonstrate its cost-effectiveness with hard numbers—especially when it comes to asking for last year's budget to be matched.

From launch day onwards, your program leaders should invest time in building a multi-aspect business case to prove its value to your C-level Marketing, Sales, HR, and Financial executives.

Their overall goal will be to show that when it comes to building your company's brand and connecting with both prospective and existing clients, employee advocacy is far and away the most cost-effective method.

Creating Your Business Case for Employee Advocacy: Key Metrics To Focus On

Marketing

Comparing your corporate social media following with your advocates' social media following will allow your program leaders to show the greater reach and impact of advocacy.

Sales

Your program leaders should curate impressive anecdotes about your advocates' social media activity generating leads and closing sales.

HR

Your program's leaders will be able to show the employer brand benefits of your advocacy program by comparing the average number of resumes submitted for open roles before your program's launch with the average number submitted after its launch.

Finance

For the CFO's benefit, your program's leaders should focus on ROI. Avoid fluffy numbers and demonstrate how much employee advocacy has saved your company in advertising spend, and directly contributed to new business through employee-generated referrals.

LEVEL 8:

CAREER MODE

97.
KEEP THE PROS CLOSE!: NETWORK WITH OTHER STAKEHOLDERS.

It's likely there are many people in your company who will see significant value in employees sharing content. These people will have a vested interest in your program. Finding them will benefit your program immensely.

If your advocacy program is going to be large, you'll need to involve people from other business units and geographies.

Talking to sales directors who manage large teams can be a great way to onboard vast swathes of employees. They'll have the teams and the use cases—you'll only need to connect the dots for them.

The same goes for HR directors and talent attraction leaders. Bringing them into the fold early will have a huge, positive impact on your employer brand and hiring.

Don't make advocacy just another daily task. Create a community around your program—perhaps in Microsoft Teams or Slack—so advocates and department leaders can share their successes and learn from one another.

WHO ARE THE KEY STAKEHOLDERS WITH A VESTED INTEREST IN EMPLOYEE ADVOCACY SUCCESS?

Marketing

Their goal? Increase brand awareness, social media engagement, drive website traffic, generate marketing-qualified leads.

The C-Suite

Their goal? See return-on-investment, reach business goals, be seen as an industry thought leader and a great employer.

Sales

Their goal? Increase leads and conversions, position sales team as industry experts, improve social selling.

HR & Recruitment

Their goal? Attract the right talent, reduce time-to-hire and cost-to-hire. Be seen as a great employer with excellent company culture.

98.
THE PATH TO PROMOTION: USE THIS AS A CAREER LAUNCHPAD.

So, you're launching an employee advocacy program. It's likely that the concept is completely new to your company. Or perhaps advocacy was happening organically on a small scale, and you're looking to grow this activity and turn it into an official program.

Either way, you're the person who is taking the initiative to build this thing. The opportunity for your own career is huge. When you drive a huge spike in social media engagement, you have the potential to become internally famous at your organization.

Use the opportunity to network internally, and become known as someone who gets things done. Whether you're looking for a promotion, or for external career opportunities, it's a sure-fire way to increase your visibility.

If people in your company don't know who you are, they certainly will when you deliver results.

If you're using technology, you'll have a wealth of data at your fingertips. These stats tell a compelling story. Use social media to tell it! Share your journey from starting to scaling your program, and inspire others to do the same.

WHEN YOU DRIVE A HUGE SPIKE IN SOCIAL MEDIA ENGAGEMENT, YOU HAVE THE POTENTIAL TO BECOME INTERNALLY FAMOUS AT YOUR ORGANIZATION.

99.
YOU'RE NOT ALONE!: NETWORK WITH PROGRAM LEADERS FROM OTHER COMPANIES.

While advocacy used to be a fringe idea, it's becoming more mainstream. These days, you'll see people adding "Employee Advocacy Program Manager" to their LinkedIn bios or work experience.

Following and networking with other program leaders will further your understanding of the employee advocacy and employer branding space overall, as well as spark content and strategy ideas.

Don't be afraid to reach out to them and have a conversation. As long as they're not direct competitors, most employee advocacy program managers will be down to share their insights.

Take a look at the content their advocates are sharing. Knowing what other companies are doing well, and what might not be working will help you manage your own advocacy program.

You don't need to reinvent the wheel when it comes to building your strategy.

Bradley Keenan 🏆 (He/Him)
Founder & CEO of DSMN8. The Employee Influencer Platform. Grow ...
6d · 🌐

Employee advocacy program leaders: you're not alone!

Advocacy used to be a fringe idea, but it's becoming more mainstream.

Use this to your advantage. Follow and network with other program leaders on LinkedIn.

Not only will you further your understanding of employee advocacy and employer branding in general, but you can learn from their content and strategy.

Take a look at the content their advocates share. What's working well? There's no need to reinvent the wheel when it comes to creating your own advocacy strategy.

Don't just be a lurker, reach out and start a conversation. Most employee advocacy program managers are down to share their insights!

100.
GOT RESOURCES? READ THEM...
AND THEN READ THEM AGAIN.

Though employee advocacy is a relatively young industry, plenty of great companies have been involved for years, creating some amazing resources you can use to improve your program.

Don't assume every white paper produced is actually a sales brochure disguised as thought leadership. Ultimately, employee advocacy companies want success for their clients, so whether you use technology or not, they'll likely contain excellent insights to help your program get the best possible results.

You should make any such insights readily available to your advocates to help them learn more. Information about social selling, thought leadership, or just general social media best practices will be incredibly useful to them.

You can also use your resource area to host your social media policy, share guidance on internal processes, explain any technology you may be using, and clarify what content you'd like advocates to share. Create your own resources too!

Your employees learn in different ways and at different speeds, so providing access to all the information they might need to become successful advocates is the best policy. That way, they can approach it in their own way and at their own speed.

EXPLORE MY RESOURCE HUB TO FIND:

- eBooks and white papers to help you get the most from your advocacy program.
- Templates, including a social media policy, survey on employee social media use, and an employee advocacy training plan.
- Tools, including ROI and reach calculators.
- Blog posts, podcast episodes, masterclasses, and case studies from organizations in a variety of industries.

101.

LEARN FROM THE BEST!:
CASE STUDIES ARE YOUR FRIENDS.

While employee advocacy is relatively new, it's not brand new. The EA industry has been around for a good few years now. This means there are lots of case studies and examples you can learn from.

It's worth taking the time to read any employee advocacy case study you can get your hands on. These examples will help you build your strategy, maximize the results of your program, and help you avoid the pitfalls that others weren't so lucky to miss.

With this knowledge, you'll be better prepared to handle any issues that may arise and make informed decisions when it comes to scaling your program.

Don't just do this at the beginning of your employee advocacy journey. Never stop learning. For success on social media, you need to stay ahead of the curve. It's a fast-moving industry! As more companies lean into employee advocacy, more case studies will become available, and you never know when you'll discover a new tactic to try out.

It's also a great way to find others in the industry to connect with, who could become valuable members of your network.

SUCCESS STORIES

Find out how DSMN8 clients achieved employee advocacy success. Learn about their challenges, how we helped overcome them, and see the results they achieved.

QUIZ: ARE YOU READY FOR EMPLOYEE ADVOCACY?

Employee advocacy IS for everyone, but it helps to know you've got the foundations in place first.

		YES	NO	
01	DO YOU HAVE A SOCIAL MEDIA POLICY?	☐	☐	

		YES	NO	N/A
02	IF SO, DOES YOUR SOCIAL MEDIA POLICY ENCOURAGE SAFE SOCIAL MEDIA USE?	☐	☐	☐

		YES	NO	
03	DO YOU HAVE SOMEONE TO RUN THIS THING? THIS COULD BE YOU!	☐	☐	
04	CAN YOU GET C-LEVEL SPONSORSHIP? IN SHORT, WILL THEY BACK THIS THING AND USE IT THEMSELVES?	☐	☐	
05	ARE YOU TRYING TO INCREASE YOUR WEBSITE TRAFFIC?	☐	☐	
06	IS YOUR GLASSDOOR RATING ABOVE 3.5 STARS?	☐	☐	
07	ARE YOUR EMPLOYEES CURRENTLY USING SOCIAL MEDIA FOR WORK PURPOSES?	☐	☐	
08	ARE YOU POSTING TO YOUR OWN PROFESSIONAL SOCIAL MEDIA (E.G. LINKEDIN) MORE THAN ONCE PER MONTH?	☐	☐	
09	IS YOUR COMPANY PRODUCING MORE THAN 2 PIECES OF CONTENT PER WEEK?	☐	☐	

Your Results:

Ticked Yes 1-3 Times?
Based on your answers, it seems that this wouldn't be the best time to launch a program, but that doesn't mean you won't get there! Start by creating an advocacy-ready social media policy (chapter 6), and work on making great content that employees will want to share (chapter 17).

Ticked Yes 4-5 Times?
Sure, there's work to be done. But don't worry, all hope is not lost. Sometimes, you just need to go back to basics and look at ways to get good foundations in place. Start by reviewing chapter 5: Failing To Plan Is Planning To Fail... and create your game plan!

Ticked Yes 6-8 Times?
It sounds like you're almost good to go! You're prepared to implement the strategies in this book, but there are still a few areas to improve on. Refer to chapter 12 and create your ideal advocate profiles, then create content tailored to them. If you'd like a bit more support to give yourself a head start, I've got you. Feel free to reach out to me on LinkedIn.

Ticked Yes 9 Times?
Amazing! This suggests that you are in very good shape. You have the content, the culture, and the skills to lead a world-class employee advocacy initiative. Go and smash it.

CONCLUSION.

Whether you've read this book cover-to-cover or flipped through to read tips at random, I hope you have taken value from it.

If you take away just one thing from everything we've covered, let it be this:

Employee advocacy is not hard, you just need to have a clear strategy and specific goals.

The results will come, as long as you get the fundamentals in place.

Think about it this way: a car is only useful with a driver behind the wheel and fuel in the tank.

Your advocacy program needs to be nurtured. You need to put in the effort to onboard advocates, scale your program, and provide regular content for them to share.

People-powered social isn't the future, it's now. That mindset shift must be communicated throughout your organization, from senior leadership right down to your interns. Employee advocacy needs to become a key part of your company culture.

GET EARLY ACCESS TO THE EMPLOYEE ADVOCACY COURSE

Readers of my book can get free early access to my course: Employee Advocacy 101, the "Mini MBA" in employee advocacy.

Become your organization's employee advocacy expert, and demonstrate your skills by becoming certified.

What's included?

- 12 on-demand video modules.
- Supporting resources for every module.
- Test your knowledge with end-of-module assessments.
- Get certified in Employee Advocacy!

ABOUT THE AUTHOR.

Bradley Keenan is a British technology entrepreneur, CEO, and co-founder of DSMN8, the All-in-One Employee Advocacy Platform. Bradley has built three leading B2B marketing technology companies, used by over 1,000 of the world's leading brands.

While integrating his company, E-Tale, into their new publicly-owned parent company after acquisition, he noticed a considerable divide between sales and marketing.

Marketing produced great content, but very few employees shared it. Bradley identified this as a waste of valuable energy, creativity, and resources, and sought to provide a solution to bridge the gap. That's when DSMN8 was brought to life.

FURTHER RESOURCES.

- **DSMN8 Resource Hub:**
  https://dsmn8.com/resource-hub/
- **The Employee Advocacy & Influence Podcast:**
  dsmn8.com/the-employee-advocacy-podcast/
- **The DSMN8 Blog:**
  https://dsmn8.com/dsmn8-blog/
- **Social Media Policy Template:**
  dsmn8.com/resources/social-media-policy-template/
- **Employee Advocacy ROI Calculator:**
  dsmn8.com/employee-advocacy-roi-calculator/
- **Guide To The First 60 Days of Employee Advocacy:**
  dsmn8.com/blog/the-first-60-days-employee-advocacy/

Follow DSMN8 on LinkedIn for the latest employee advocacy tips, hints, and best practices.

linkedin.com/company/dsmn8

Printed in Great Britain
by Amazon

43467142R00136